W9-BPM-595

Praise for *Brief Encounters*

"Funny and poignant stories and essays about his life, his career, family, politics—it's all here. So intelligent and witty and charming and innocent. Kind of like Dick Cavett himself. So sit back, relax, and enjoy this book. I know I did."

—from the Foreword by Jimmy Fallon

"*Brief Encounters* includes numerous observations about contemporary culture and politics—neither Democrats nor Republicans are spared—as well as moving recollections of and tributes to stars no longer with us, from Stan Laurel to James Gandolfini."

—*USA Today*

"The twenty-eight-year host of *The Dick Cavett Show*—one of twentieth-century America's first media forums for entertainment culture—shares his recollections of the famous figures he encountered throughout his career. Fifty-six years after the debut of his talk show, Cavett . . . remains as quick-witted and bold-minded as ever."

—*Entertainment Weekly*

"[Cavett's] book is at its best when summoning memories of long-gone entertainment figures such as Stan Laurel and Groucho Marx. . . . Cavett never abandons his wit. . . . With his pithy prose style and compact paragraphs, Cavett has a sure feel for the art of column-writing."

—*The Columbus Dispatch*

"Hugely engaging . . . [Cavett] was the most intellectually credible and culturally aware comedian ever to have an American talk show."

—*The Buffalo News*

"This collection of columns from Cavett's online column in *The New York Times* will appeal mostly to people over sixty, and especially to those over seventy, inasmuch as the affable former talk-show host is at his best when he's reminiscing about show-business luminaries of the '60s and '70s, folks such as Art Linkletter, Groucho Marx, Arthur Godfrey, and Tony Curtis, though Steve Jobs and James Gandolfini also make appearances."   —*Toronto Star*

"The book is a delightful peek behind the curtain at celebrities, complex characters, and the nuances of everyday life—all told with his singular wit and style."   —*Publishers Weekly*

"The very model of a quick-witted interviewer, Cavett . . . still works the crowd effectively. . . . [Cavett] remembers working as a gag writer for famed comedians and recalls the Broadway badinage and smart repartee that marked the well-regarded *Dick Cavett Show*."
                                                                —*Kirkus Reviews*

"With his signature wit, writer and comic Cavett shares 'brief encounters' from his early childhood in Nebraska on through his career in show business . . . [Cavett] expound[s] on life, American culture, and politics with obvious love of magic, entertainment, and words."   —*Booklist*

BRIEF
ENCOUNTERS

ALSO BY DICK CAVETT

Talk Show:
Confrontations, Pointed Commentary,
and Off-Screen Secrets

Eye on Cavett
(with Christopher Porterfield)

Cavett
(with Christopher Porterfield)

BRIEF ENCOUNTERS

Conversations, Magic Moments, and Assorted Hijinks

DICK CAVETT

Foreword by **Jimmy Fallon**

A New York Times Book
St. Martin's Griffin
New York

BRIEF ENCOUNTERS. Copyright © 2014 by Richard A. Cavett.
Foreword © 2014 by Jimmy Fallon. All rights reserved. Printed in
the United States of America. For information, address
St. Martin's Press, 175 Fifth Avenue, New York, N.Y. 10010.

www.stmartins.com

The essays in this book originally appeared, in slightly different
form, on the Web site of *The New York Times,* which owns
the copyright jointly with the author.

Designed by Meryl Sussman Levavi

The Library of Congress has cataloged the Henry Holt edition as follows:

Cavett, Dick.
    Brief encounters : conversations, magic moments, and assorted hijinks
/ Dick Cavett ; foreword by Jimmy Fallon.—First edition.
        p. cm.
    Includes index.
    ISBN 978-0-8050-9977-5 (hardcover)
    ISBN 978-0-8050-9978-2 (e-book)
    1. Cavett, Dick. 2. Television personalities—United States—
Biography. 3. Entertainers—United States—Biography. 4. Dick Cavett
show (Television program) I. Title.
    PN2287.C38A3 2014
    791.4502'8092—dc23
    [B]

                                                              2014006409

ISBN 978-1-250-07075-3 (trade paperback)

Our books may be purchased in bulk for promotional, educational, or
business use. Please contact your local bookseller or the Macmillan
Corporate and Premium Sales Department at (800) 221-7945, extension
5442, or by e-mail at MacmillanSpecialMarkets@macmillan.com.

First published by Henry Holt and Company, LLC

First St. Martin's Griffin Edition: October 2015

10 9 8 7 6 5 4 3 2 1

To the readers of the New York Times *online Opinion*

pages, especially those who have written such erudite and

entertaining responses to my columns.

If you want to leave responses to this book, you may do

so at www.dickcavettshow.com. I'll read every one of them.

(Five points off for spelling.)

Contents

Foreword by Jimmy Fallon

The first time I spoke to the great Dick Cavett was the night before my very first show as the new host of *Late Night*. I was nervous and excited and scared and happy all at the same time. I had no idea what I was about to go through. And then, out of the blue, I got a phone call from Dick Cavett.

I couldn't believe it. Dick Cavett! From *The Dick Cavett Show*. This is the guy who interviewed John Lennon and Yoko Ono. This is the guy who refereed the classic argument between Norman Mailer and Gore Vidal. This is the guy who, when Mailer taunted him by saying, "Why don't you look at your question sheet and ask a question?" responded, "Why don't you fold it five ways and put it where the moon don't shine?" And here I was talking to him. Whaaaaaaaaat?

Well, he couldn't have been nicer and more generous. He said he was rooting for me and wished me luck hosting the show, and I'll never forget the advice he gave me. (I think it was about listening to people when they talk. Or something like that.) By the end of the call he had calmed me down and made me feel better. Then I asked him for his number and he told me to "write it down on a piece of paper, fold it five ways, and put it where the moon don't shine."

Anyway, it was also during that phone call that he first told me he was writing these stories that would eventually become this book. Funny and poignant stories and essays about his life, his career, family, politics—it's all here. So intelligent and witty and charming and innocent. Kind of like Dick Cavett himself. So sit back, relax, and enjoy this book. I know I did. I mean, I love books. Don't you just love books? I love the way they feel. The way they smell. Of course, I read them mostly on a Kindle now. But I still miss the *smell* of books. Hey!—I just thought of something. Maybe they should invent a *candle* that smells like a book. That way you can light the candle before you start reading your Kindle, and it'll smell like you're reading in a library. They can call it the "Kindle Candle." Wow! That's a great idea. Can I trademark that??? Holy crap. I'm gonna be rich!!! I have to call my lawyer.

Okay, enjoy *Brief Encounters*. And Dick, if you're reading this, let me know if you want in on the ground floor of the Kindle Candle™ thing. Either way, call me. I haven't heard from you since my first show five years ago.

JIMMY

BRIEF ENCOUNTERS

Dreams, Let Up on Us!

Will Shakespeare told us, in that line always misquoted with the word "of"—even by Bogey in *The Maltese Falcon*—that "we are such stuff as dreams are made on." If they're in fact what we're made on, it's a mixed blessing.

We know that much of Freud's work has been repudiated and disparaged by the psychiatric world. Particularly his dream symbolism. But I've seen dream analysis work. When "in treatment"—that lovely euphemism for getting your head shrunk—with the brilliant Dr. Willard Gaylin, I would come in with a mishmash of a dream and, feature by crazy feature, he would elucidate it. It was—and can we now retire this word for at least a decade, young people?—awesome.

Some people claim they never dream. There are times when I wish I were one of them.

There are two types of dream that rate, for me at least, the word "nightmare." The buggers are the Actor's Dream and the Exam Dream. If you've never endured either of these, count yourself lucky. Maybe I'm getting your share.

The question I can never find an answer to is the one that makes dreams so mysterious. When you watch a movie or read a story you don't know what's coming next. You're surprised by what happens as it unfolds. You know that someone wrote the book or made the movie.

But who in hell is the author of the dream? How can it be anyone but you? But how can it be you if it's all new to you, if you don't know what's coming? Do you write the dream, then hide it from yourself, forget it, and then "sit out front" and watch it? Everything in it is a surprise, pleasant or unpleasant. And, unlike a book or film, you can't fast-forward to see how it comes out. So where does it come from? And who "wrote" it?

(I apologize if I've led you to think I have the answers.)

What shows you the dream and at the same time blinds you to its source? The mechanism has to be ingeniously complex to pull this stunt off. But it seems that the complexity of the human brain is too, well, complex for that same brain to understand.

A nice puzzle.

I'm not sure I've ever met anyone who hasn't had the Exam Dream. (Do people who haven't been to school get this dream, or are they immune to the torture?)

There you are in the classroom, trying desperately to get a peek at someone else's paper, but they've just turned the page as you writhe in the realization that you forgot to study.

Why, this far from one's education, does one (or at least I) still get the damned dream?

Once I awoke in a sweat from it, walked around a little to shake it off, calmed down, and went back to sleep, only to be blindsided that same night by the Actor's Dream.

Every actor gets it, even people who have only been in the school play. You're backstage, about to go on, and desperately trying to find a copy of the play to get at least your first line or two, but no one has a script. How did you get to opening night and fail to learn a single line?

You're plagued with "How did I do this to myself?" and "Am I even wearing the right costume?" and "Do I go out there and try to ad-lib a part I don't know, maybe getting a few lines right by chance?" and "In a moment I'll step out there and make an ass of myself, let down and embarrass my fellow actors, and probably be fired on the spot as they give people's money back." It goes on and on and won't let up on you.

The merciful release at the much-too-late-in-coming realization "Oh, thank God, it's a dream!" leaves you limp.

Freud, "the Viennese quack" (Nabokov), is said to have pointed out that the mental agony of an excruciating dream is always far worse than the real situation would be.

It's true.

Logic tells you that in waking real life you probably wouldn't get into the situation you lie there suffering and blaming yourself for. The rich variety of hateful anxiety dreams can be about anything: not having studied; having lost your passport in an unfamiliar land; getting hopelessly lost in the woods; being late for and unable to find your own wedding; having let your pet get lost; and the myriad other sleeping torture plots the mind is heir to.

The psychic pain is acute. And even if these things did happen, awful as they would be, why must the psychic pain be ten times more excruciating in the dream than it would be in real life?

Who does this to us? Who or what is the sadistic force operating on us here? It's hard to admit, but doesn't it have to be ourselves?

Then why are we doing it to ourselves? What did we do to deserve it? And does it all stand for something about us that's so awful it has to be disguised as something else in the dream?

Please have your answers to these questions on my desk by Friday. Neatness and clarity of presentation will count, and five points will be taken off for spelling.

Time for a laugh here. I just remembered that the great Robert Benchley wrote, somewhere, a piece about that aspect of dreams that's common to most of them—that nothing is quite itself as you know it. "It's my house but it's not my house. It's my gray suit but it has wheels on it."

Should you deem this subject worthy of a return visit, I'll expose the specific anxiety dreams I collected for a time from some famous people: Laurence Olivier, Rudolf Nureyev, others. (Or you can just tell me to shut up about it.)

APRIL 30, 2010

The Windows of the Soul Need Cleaning

I'm bowled almost over by how many readers replied so intelligently, and revealingly, on this subject: the mystery of dreams and dreaming.

I asked a learnèd friend about this: Dr. Jay Meltzer, the legendary physician to whom I went for medicine until he retired and to whom I still go for his culinary gifts and for education and tutoring on tough subjects.

He said that this whole area—the workings of the brain—is the next great frontier of discovery, following upon such achieved milestones as the genome, molecular biology, Darwin and evolution, etc. (Some, not fully grasping the subject, might add to the milestone list the microchip, video games, and Viagra.)

Meltzer talked about the super-miraculous validation of the fact that the myriad separate circuits of the brain talk to one another. And without our being in on the conversation. Probably just as well that we can't hear what they say about us.

This plays into my question last time to which so many readers responded, about how a dream can be, so to speak, written and produced and "played" before us without our being in on its creation. If we're just the viewer, who is the dream's author?

Meltzer tied in with this the fascinating distinction between the thing that makes us human creatures unique—consciousness—and simple awareness. A dog is not conscious. He is aware, but only we are conscious. (You're tempted to say some are more conscious than others, but let that pass.)

Hearing an intellectual shtarker like Meltzer talk about such stuff makes me want to go back to school. He's greatly interesting about how we all have two brains: the rational brain and the irrational brain. Not to get sidetracked from dreams here, but for an oversimplified example: the rational brain knows not to smoke.

Philosophy's heavy hitters have also addressed this subject, calling attention to the nature of dreaming and its kinship with madness. I've been haunted since college by Baudelaire's—wasn't it?—"I have felt the wind of the wing of madness pass over me." Insanity and dreams share many things, among them disordered thought and, of course, hallucination. As Artie Schopenhauer (so I'm a name-dropper) had it, "A dream is a short-lasting psychosis, and a psychosis is a long-lasting dream." Could Soupy Sales have put it better?

Does anything show the complexity of the miraculous brain more than that weird curiosity, the sleep-protection dream? In Freud's native tongue, probably something like *Schlafschutzentraum*.

In my day, Yale still had the torture of the 8:00 a.m. class. At that age everything in you is opposed to early wake-up, and I would either be late for class or miss it completely—by dreaming I was there. Nice of the dream mechanism, letting you sleep, except for the consequences. The complex mechanism is so proficient and intricate in its work that that specific dream can even defy rigorous testing. In the dream itself, and even in class, I would ask myself if this were the dream—or the class.

Once, I knew full well I was in class, but tested it anyway. There's Cecil Lang, the professor. (One said "Mr. Lang" at Yale.) Here's Chris Porterfield at my right elbow, there's Dave Greenway in the back, and this is my desk. I gripped it solidly and it passed the test. I felt silly. And sillier a moment later. When I woke up. In bed.

This shook me. (Is there any chance I'm dreaming I'm typing this now?)

A number of readers reported that awful thing where you're trying to escape something, physically, and you can't get going. The muscles have turned to jelly and your nerves are shot. Tell me ASAP, what is this dream protecting?

And does each profession have its own style of anxiety dream? Does the trial lawyer in court, embarking on cross-examination, look down to find that instead of his notes he has brought a book of Sudoku? Does the brain surgeon find in midoperation that instead of his scalpel he is holding a limp stick of Bonomo's Turkish Chewing Taffy? (Phallic symbolism?) Feel free to submit examples from your own particular trade.

Lest I forget, I teased you last time by promising a couple of specimens of celeb anxiety dreams I've heard. (I know you can't slander the dead, but do I dishonor them by revealing their dreams? Let's say no.)

Laurence Olivier's punisher was particularly cruel:

"It's not, dear boy, that I don't know my lines. It's far worse than that. I'm standing backstage, waiting for my cue. I hear it and open the door to make my entrance.

"But the door doesn't lead to the set. It leads instead to a room full of tools. And two more doors. I open one. It leads to another pair of doors.

"I frantically fling one open. Good God! It leads to a whole row of doors. I am soaked in sweat.

"As I keep flinging open one damned door after the other, I can hear my fellow actors out onstage, desperately ad-libbing and wondering where the hell I am.

"My wife says I wake up screaming."

Olivier's story may have been, as they say, "in conversation." (Even if not, what fun it is to say that.) Rudolf Nureyev's nightmare was told either on my show or over his nightly after-show steak tartare in the formerly great Russian Tea Room.

Poor Rudolf's dream (*Traum*, appropriately, in German) contained the standard ingredients of the devilish one in which one is poorly prepared and horribly confused. In his case, he is on the great stage, dancing, and suddenly realizes he's lost and doesn't know the rest of the choreography.

He desperately tries to recall rehearsal but can't. "Was I even at rehearsal?"

He is fumbling the steps. Panicked, he begins to sweat, and hears laughter from the audience. The performance grinds to a stop and his fellow dancers "—and George Balanchine!—are glaring at me."

Then comes the punch line:

"Pouring out sweat, I look down. I am wearing my street shoes!"

MAY 14, 2010

Art Did the Darndest Things . . . to Your Jokes

The voice of the editor wondered if, instead of the column I would have handed in this time, I might want to do a short, quick appreciation of Art Linkletter. My only reluctance in accepting the mission is that what I have to offer may not be everyone's idea of an appreciation.

I wrote for Linkletter for a week for the same reason that I wrote for a lot of famous people for a week or two only. My boss-to-be, Johnny Carson, was canny enough not to replace my then former boss Jack Paar immediately upon Jack's exit from *The Tonight Show* in 1962. There may have also been a contract obligation elsewhere that kept him from doing so. Even if so, the wise thing for Carson was not to appear to jump into Jack's chair while people were still lamenting Jack's departure.

My guess is that the gap between the two stars was bigger than most anyone remembers. Following Jack came a kind of summer stock season for *Tonight*. Entertainers of all kinds, shapes, and degrees of talent hosted the show. I recall Robert Cummings, Donald O'Connor, Mort Sahl, Merv Griffin (a newcomer), possibly a Gabor, Steve & Eydie, Jack E. Leonard, Jack Carter, Sam Levenson (smashing), Jerry Lewis, and two memorable weeks of Groucho.

For some reason, and partly because Jack had established it, each felt the need to do The Monologue.

The results were mixed.

Linkletter was a man of great accomplishment and performing skill, a shrewd, shrewd businessman. His was a great American success story, complete with humble beginning. He provided the world, especially when he was working with those kids, with a million healthy laughs. Among his list of performing gifts, monology was absent.

The *Tonight Show* writing staff included, besides me, veteran writers for Bob Hope, Jack Paar, and other biggies. We had a bad week of it.

The great David Lloyd would drop on Linkletter's desk his usual gems, only to have them rejected. "And, invariably, if he picks one, he picks one of my feebs," Dave would lament. ("Feeb": Lloydese for a weak joke, thrown in, admittedly, to fill the page a bit.)

One night at dinner at Dave's house in Beverly Hills, years later when his résumé had gone on from Art Linkletter to *The Mary Tyler Moore Show* (including his Emmy-winning "Chuckles Bites the Dust" episode), *Frasier, Cheers, Taxi*, and more, he reduced the table to hysterics by recalling a specific example of what he called "how to Linkletterize a joke." So that no living being of whatever dimness could be left behind in getting it.

Ready? All that you youngies need to know is that there was once a popular comic named Jack E. Leonard, a man physically rotund enough to be appropriately, and affectionately, called "Fat Jack."

Here is the one line Art selected from that day's Dave Lloyd submissions: "On tonight's show we're going to talk about comedy teams. You know, comedy teams like Laurel and Hardy, Abbott and Costello, Martin and Lewis, Jack E. Leonard. . . ."

That's how Dave wrote it.

Here's what Art—democratically ensuring that no one hearing it should be left in the dark—did to it. All emphases are his:

"On tonight's show we're going to talk about comedy teams. You know, comedy teams like Laurel and Hardy, Abbott and Costello, Martin and Lewis . . . and *big fat* Jack E. Leonard . . . who's *so* fat, he's a *one-man* comedy team . . . *all by himself!*"

The audience reaction? If someone had dropped a pin, it would have been deafening.

That did it. Rather than for us to go on strike for the remaining days of that week, I suggested a plan. I went downstairs in the RCA building to the bookstore, bought a Bennett Cerf joke book, and we each copied jokes out and handed them in. None of us could bear to find out what fate they met.

Someone, I guarantee, will react to this with the prerecorded "How can you speak disrespectfully of the dead?" Truth is, I have always found it remarkably easy. Why anyone, by dying, should thereby be declared beyond criticism, innocent of wrongdoing, suddenly filled with virtue, and above reproach escapes me. And the minor crime of smothering jokes hardly puts Art Linkletter in the pantheon of history's malefactors.

He was a pleasant and cordial man to be around, and inspiringly professional.

I don't know how well he knew his Shakespeare, but he paid three times the grievous penalty expressed in Old Montague's "O thou untaught! What manners is in this? To press before thy father to a grave?"

It happened to Art Linkletter with three of his five children. A price even an envious Greek god might consider too high to exact for such success.

MAY 28, 2010

A. Godfrey: A Man for a Long, Long Season

You may feel that this column should bear the cautionary label "Warning: Oldies Only."

Because its subject is largely forgotten.

The astute Andy Rooney, who worked for him, predicted that despite decades of huge stardom, Godfrey would be forgotten, adding that his effect on broadcasting would be indelible.

He was a colossus of the entertainment world to a degree that may never be equaled; if only for the fact that he had—count 'em—three network shows at the same time on CBS: a simulcast talk show in the morning, and not one but two (live) prime-time shows every week, consistently in the top ten.

Arthur Godfrey was not just an entertainer. If the phrase ever applied to a human being, he was an industry.

Advertisers so craved his then revolutionary and greatly successful practice of personally delivering, live and ad lib, each and every commercial that sponsors waited in line. He was the top salesman in radio and television—so it is said. So large was his take for the network on his morning show that it was avowed in the ad industry that by the time William Paley (Mr. CBS) finished his breakfast, Arthur had paid the network's bills for the day.

He had vowed he would never praise any product he didn't totally and genuinely believe in; ironic in the case of the unfiltered Chesterfields with which he was virtually synonymous in the public mind and ear as he intoned the words, "Chesterfields . . . they satisfy." As he was first to later admit, they also helped kill him, and his guilt over urging them on the populace stayed with him.

Somehow he took a shine to me when I was but a struggling comedian in Greenwich Village and had me on the remnant of his career, the morning radio show. He would have to press the "cough" button frequently, muttering "Damn this emphysema" before releasing it.

Starting out from less than nowhere, he achieved immense fame, wealth, and success, and lived well past the eventual fading of his epic-length career. In his later years, he self-educated himself (as he had in everything, having had no schooling) on a whole new subject: he became an ardent—and effective—ecologist. He repented in later life about what his enthusiastic boosting of the charms of Florida ultimately (over)did to the area. On the accompanying video he mentions first hearing the word "ecology."

(Speaking of aviation, by the time he died he had piloted every variety of military aircraft except, to his great regret, a jet helicopter.)

Godfrey's vigorous opposition, on a show of mine, to the development of the then controversial Supersonic Transport and what it would do to the atmosphere ("We need that gook in the atmosphere about as much as we need another bag of those clunkers from the moon") contributed mightily to the pollution of my relations with the Nixon White House. (For creepy verification see YouTube's "Pres. Nixon Wants Revenge Against Talk Show Host Dick Cavett.")

Although other guests had denounced the SST on my show, losing Godfrey, aviation's great supporter and practitioner ("When Arthur's not on the air, he's in it"—Fred Allen), was one too many for the resident criminal of Pennsylvania Avenue.

John Gilroy, my late producer, came into my office a bit shaken. "Guess what," he said. "The Nixon White House keeps a scorecard on our show." A grim and humorless voice on the phone, heralded by the chilling words "White House calling," had informed John that they had counted the times the SST had been denounced on the

Cavett show, were seriously miffed, and would be sending a spokes-man to praise the SST.

Having my show booked from the White House produced an eerie sensation. It was subtly suggested that Mr. Cavett would, of course, be nice to him.

They sent a crew-cut gent—Nixon liked, in his words, "real men"—named Magruder (not the W-gate one, Jeb). With bone-breaking attempted amiability, Magruder was permitted to do his pitch for the SST, uninterrupted by his, with difficulty, amiable host. When he had said his piece, I thanked him, made clear to the viewers that he had been booked by the White House's own talent agency, and merely added the few words, "I certainly hope the SST is defeated. But thanks for being here, Mr. . . . . Magruder, is it?"

The fan was hit. The city of D.C. was not delighted with D.C.

The Great Unindicted Co-Conspirator (in one of his favorite illegalities) saw that my entire staff was audited, cruelly in the cases of the lesser-paid ones. This, combined with my formal protest of the administration's attempt to deport John Lennon (henchman H. R. Haldeman, more in tune with pop culture than his boss, had poured into Nixon's ear, "This guy Lennon could sway an election") made me *persona* less than *grata* at the famous address. Hard to believe I was once earlier invited to a big Nixon do in the East Room—cordially greeted by henchman Haldeman and by Henry Kissinger, in the days before permanently sullying my welcome with the gang.

Much journalistic ink was spilled over the Magruder show, and Arthur called. "Sorry, Richard, if I made trouble for you." The famous chuckle followed my assuring him I'd enjoyed every minute of it.

(Going through an old box of accreted stuff the other day, I was reminded that each time I had Arthur on a show he immediately penned a cordial thank-you note.)

In my improbable life, which has included meeting nearly all my heroes and heroines in show business and in many other fields, meeting Arthur Godfrey strained credulity. It seemed only a few years earlier that he emerged from our old Majestic slow-to-warm-up radio five days a week, while I was a schoolkid in Nebraska. When I interviewed him, I told him that on a scorching Great Plains summer day, without air-conditioning, you could stroll past house after house and hear, through June-bug-inhabited screens, the amiable voice, uninterrupted.

When he came on the set, I was often struck by the vigor of Arthur's entrance. With effort, his limp was not noticeable. The briskness was an act, having to do with the strong will of a man smashed to pieces in a head-on car crash in his younger days. After six months in the hospital, he defied the medics' assurance that he would spend the rest of his life in a wheelchair; in middle age—on chronically painful injured hips and knees—he learned to ice-skate.

You may have to excuse me now. This column is due and, with the A/C on the fritz, the act of typing is producing moist secretion. (I hope you're not eating.) So may I close, for now, on a subject I hope will be a pleasant nostalgia trip for many readers old enough to remember Pearl Harbor?

P.S. Thanks for valuable info on Arthur to a man who survived the sometimes stormy seas of being his longtime agent, Peter Kelley, and to Arthur J. Singer for his excellent book, *Arthur Godfrey: The Adventures of an American Broadcaster.*

JUNE 25, 2010

More of Our Man Godfrey

I'm glad to see how many readers liked revisiting—or visiting for the first time—Arthur Godfrey.

He's one more reminder of the infinite possible varieties of human being. I never met or heard of anyone remotely like him.

The arc of his life brings to mind the old phrase "American success story": disintegrated family, poverty, scuffling for food and lodging, body smashed in head-on crash, cancer survivor, and a career that brought fame and fortune beyond his dreams. And then a kind of rebirth in later life as an ardent and effective ecologist and conservationist before either word was widely known.

And, ultimately, fade-out from the public mind.

Readers, last time, asked about the Julius La Rosa incident, a notorious happening that, back then, seemed to be the hottest news subject of the time.

Its damage threatened to bring down the Godfrey colossus, and it never entirely went away.

There are two versions. One is that Arthur heartlessly, publicly fired a personable young singer—a member of the Godfrey "family"—live, on the air. So great was Godfrey's size in the entertainment world that the dramatic phrase "the nation was shocked" is no exaggeration.

In fact, reexamining the incident, it's hardly the unmitigated evil it was depicted as at the time. Not only had Godfrey and La Rosa previously talked about the young lad's desire to move on, but the big bosses at CBS strongly urged Arthur to handle the parting on the air. Doing so, Arthur used the words "Julie's swan song" and wished La Rosa well. Listening to it now, it seems both harmless and cordial.

And yet it was treated in the press as if La Rosa had been shot dead in a public square.

Godfrey's later reference to Julie's lost "humility" was a verbal blunder that some Godfrey hounders in the press blew up to the size of Pearl Harbor. (In the video clip, you will see Arthur allude to—but not refer to—"a couple of bad incidents.")

Then there's the anti-Semitism matter. At its most fulsome, it goes, "Don't you know Godfrey owned a hotel in Florida with a sign out front that read 'No Dogs or Jews'?" Although purest nonsense, you can still hear it resurrected by seniors from that era.

Unreported was the fact that although he did patronize that hotel, he made a point of checking in with Jewish friends and cast members.

He later bought into the place and abolished the odious policy. Being labeled an anti-Semite was a bum rap that those who knew the man say he emphatically did not deserve. The hotel in question, The Kenilworth, became nationally famous at the time. (I don't know if it still exists—renamed, perhaps, The Mel Gibson?)

The attacks on Arthur—and on other media giants over time—bring to mind that dreary cliché about how "the press likes to build you way up, just so they can later tear you down."

This dumbbell notion has been around since I learned to read and has the durability of the great pyramid at Giza. Sure, there's plenty of schadenfreude (all four syllables, please) around, but it's not evil press monsters who, like those envying Greek gods, like to see the mighty tumble; it's us. Envious us.

(Sorry. Subject for another time?)

Godfrey's career ran its course. But it was a marathon.

If you closed your eyes and just listened to his voice, you could see why that God-given instrument seduced a nation. He had the women of this country (exceptions, of course) in the palm of his hand.

Look at what he provided them. A nice, warm, friendly man in their life, reliable and consistently there. Thoughtful and comfortable to be with.

And best of all, he spoke directly, individually, and personally to them. Not to a mass audience, but to them, right there in their home.

This was Godfrey's genius insight. For months in the hospital after the car crash that broke nearly everything, he had only his radio as companion. And something always seemed wrong. Why, he wondered, didn't it occur to someone somewhere in broadcasting to talk to *him*?

What was really a revolutionary insight was born as the thought: Who the hell is "Ladies and gentlemen of the radio audience" supposed to reach? And who out there feels greeted by "Hello, everybody"? Who feels included in "All of our listeners out there in radio land"? Had it never occurred to anyone, he wondered, to talk only to him? Had they never heard of the magic word "you"?

When Arthur got back to work, he launched his revolutionary notion by saying into the microphone the simple phrase "How are you?" And a nation of listeners felt, for the first time, "That man is talking to me!"

My grandmother knew full well that Arthur was speaking, privately and confidentially, to her. So did millions.

Steve Allen said that Arthur revolutionized broadcasting with that one perception. Not entirely. Smart broadcasters like Allen and others picked up on and emulated it; and yet it remains surprisingly unlearned. Morning show hosts, news anchors, eyewitless news teams and cohosts—whose gallery of ad-lib reactions to startling or funny items consists of "How about that?" and "There you go"—still say, "Hi, everybody." Thereby, paradoxically, leaving out everybody.

The strong and priceless quality Arthur conveyed to the listener was always referred to as "human warmth." (Think what trouble we might be in if Rush Limbaugh had it.)

A closing note for now. Arthur had enemies. And detractors galore. And Peter Kelley, his agent and long-buffeted survivor of the Godfrey storms—once fired (temporarily) by Arthur—says, "All told, I liked him and he was my friend." And, acknowledging how difficult Arthur could be when the Vesuvian Godfrey temper boiled up, then adds something rare:

"Arthur never, never lied."

Try that sometime.

JULY 16, 2010

Real Americans, Please Stand Up

A ll this talk about the proposed mosque in Lower Manhattan reminds me of two things I heard growing up in Nebraska.

I had a sixth-grade teacher who referred to American Indians as "sneaky redskins" and our enemies in the Pacific as "dirty Japs." This abated somewhat after I asked one day in class, "Mrs. G., do you think our parents would like to know that you teach race prejudice?" She faded three shades.

The rest of that year was difficult.

As a war kid, I also heard an uncle of mine endorse a sentiment attributed to our Admiral "Bull" Halsey: "If I met a pregnant Japanese woman, I'd kick her in the belly."

These are not proud moments in my heritage. But now, I'm genuinely ashamed of us. How sad this whole mosque business is. It doesn't take much, it seems, to lift the lid and let our homegrown racism and bigotry overflow. We have collectively taken a pratfall on a moral whoopee cushion.

Surely, few of the opponents of the Islamic cultural center would feel comfortable at the "International Burn a Koran Day" planned by a southern church-supported group. (On a newscast, I think I might have even glimpsed a banner reading BRING THE WHOLE FAMILY, but maybe I was hallucinating.) This all must have gone over big on Aljazeera.

I like to think I'm not easily shocked, but here I am, seeing the emotions of the masses running like a freight train over the right to freedom of religion—never mind the rights of eminent domain and private property.

A heyday is being had by a posse of the cheesiest Republican politicos (Rick Lazio, Sarah Palin, quick-change artist John McCain, and of course the self-anointed Saint Joan of 9/11, Rudy Giuliani). Balanced, of course, by plenty of cheesy Democrats. And of course Rush Limbaugh dependably pollutes the atmosphere with his particular brand of airborne sludge.

Sad to see Harry Reid's venerable knees buckle upon seeing the vilification heaped on President Obama, and the resulting polls. (Not to suggest that this alone would cause the sudden 180-degree turn of a man of integrity facing reelection fears.)

I got invigorating jolts from the president's splendid speech—almost as good as Mayor Bloomberg's—but I was dismayed, after the worst had poured out their passionate intensity, to see him shed a few vertebrae the next day and step back.

What other churches might be objectionable because of the horrific acts of some of its members? Maybe we shouldn't have Christian churches in the South wherever the Ku Klux Klan operated because years ago self-proclaimed white Christians lynched blacks. How close to Hickam Field, at Pearl Harbor, should a Shinto shrine be allowed? I wonder how many of our young people—notorious, we are told, for their ignorance of American history—would be surprised that Japanese Americans had lives and livelihoods destroyed when they were rounded up during World War II? Should all World War II service memorials, therefore, be moved away from the sites of these internment camps?

Where does one draw the line?

I just can't believe that so many are willing to ignore the simple fact that nearly all Muslims were adamantly opposed to the actions and events that took place on 9/11 and denounced them strongly, saying that the Islamic religion in no way condones it.

Our goal in at least one of our Middle East wars is to rebuild a government in our own image—with democracy for all. Instead, we are rebuilding ourselves in the image of those who detest us. I hate to see my country—and it's a hell of a good one—endorse what we purport to hate, besmirching what distinguishes us from countries where persecution rules.

I've tried real hard to understand the objectors' position. No one is untouched by what happened on 9/11. I don't claim to be capable of imagining the anguish, grief, and anger of the people who lost their friends and loved ones that day. It really does the heart good to see that so many of *them* have denounced the outcry against the project. A fact too little reported.

And it seems to have escaped wide notice that a goodly number of Muslims died at the towers that day. (I don't mean the crazies in the planes.) What are *their* families to think of being told to beat it?

"Insulting to the dead" is a favorite phrase thrown about by opponents of the center. How about the insult to the dead American soldiers who fought at Iwo Jima and Normandy, defending American citizens abiding by the law on their own private property and exercising their freedom of religion?

Too bad that legions oppose this. A woman tells the news guy on the street, "I have absolutely no prejudice against the Muslim people. My cousin is married to one. I just don't see why they have to be here." A man complains that his opposition to the mosque is "painting me like I hate the whole Arab world." (Perhaps he dislikes them all as individuals?)

I remain amazed and really, sincerely, want to understand this. What can it be that is faulty in so many people's thought processes, their ethics, their education, their experience of life, their understanding of their country, their what-have-you, that blinds them to the fact that you can't simultaneously maintain that you have nothing against members of any religion but are willing to penalize members of this one? Can you help me with this?

Set aside for the moment that we are handing such a lethal propaganda grenade to our detractors around the world.

You can't eat this particular cake and have it, too. The true calamity, of course, is that behavior of this kind allows the enemy to win.

AUGUST 20, 2010

Dear Fellow Improbable . . .

It didn't sound like my cup of tea. In fact, it sounded like some kind of boring "think tank" thing, and I declined their nice invite.

It was Teller—of Penn &—who told me that declining was a mistake. (Yes, Teller can talk, and so could Harpo.) Teller is a brilliant man—for starters, a former Latin teacher. And what I had missed was an annual conclave of brilliant people of all varieties.

The next time, I accepted.

It's called EG (the Entertainment Gathering) and it consists of several days of one delightful talk, event, or astonishing demonstration after another. Hardly a day has passed in all these months afterward that I haven't thought about something that happened there.

It is held annually in Monterey, California, and dear Teller shot me an e-mailed tip just before I left: "Stay up late. That's when good stuff happens." This meant that after the planned events, you could find yourself in a pub hoisting an ale and chatting with a convivial circle including, say, the world's greatest clarinetist, an entertaining astrophysicist, a great magician, the physicist and mathematician Freeman Dyson, a dazzling computer artist, a juggling Karamazov Brother, a genius inventor, a most attractive woman (by trade, an astronaut), a compelling historian, and on and on; all apparently chosen for their extraordinary personalities. It seemed there was always at least one Nobel, Pulitzer, or Oscar winner in the group.

One particular speaker stands out. Not only for his genial presence but for the astounding subject matter of his talk.

But first, come back in time with me now and join me in my bathtub in Nebraska.

I'm soaping, soaking, and contemplating a film I'd just seen.

It was always fun when the teacher—in this case I must have been in about eighth grade—announced that we were "going to the movie room." Fun, even though what we usually saw would be one of those sleep-inducing ERPI classroom films with unpromising titles like *The Life of John Peter Zenger* or *Wheat Production in the Ukraine* or *The Romance of Anthracite Coal.*

But this one made everyone sit up. It was about sex. Most of us— with the suspected exception of Carolyn H.—were familiar only with the word.

There was to be no giggling.

I doubt that anyone blinked even once as we witnessed what unfolded on the screen, accompanied by the clunking of the aging 16mm projector. A few parents protested later, but most, and I suspect all, were surely relieved at being spared the chore of explaining, with weight-shifting discomfort, the facts of you-know-what.

It is all as vivid to me now as if it were yesterday. Make that today.

There was The Egg—a black ball in the center of the screen. Around it swam frantic little tadpole-like wiggly things competing to get inside. Until one did.

I doubt that any of us had heard until that instant the word "spermatozoon."

That night, in the tub, the thought hit me: "Are the little wigglers all the same? Would each one of them have resulted in me?"

I got up the courage to ask our doctor. I've never been good at admitting ignorance and probably began with "Guess what a friend of mine doesn't know the answer to?" By this subtle ruse, I got the unexpected answer. It floored me. And still does.

Back to Monterey. A genial, humorous, and brilliant geologist, and the kind of professor too few ever experience, is onstage. His name: Walter Alvarez, of the University of California, Berkeley. He and his Nobel-prized father, the late physicist Luis Alvarez, gave the world the "impact theory" that explained the demise of the dinosaurs.

Near the end of his talk, he refers to you and me as belonging to a species called "astronomically improbables."

Hasn't almost everyone, sooner or later, hit upon the realization that because you have two parents, four grandparents, eight great-grandparents, and so on into near-infinity, you are related to practically everyone on earth?

Here, for now, are just a few of Alvarez's astonishers regarding this, which made everyone gasp.

(Fundamentalists may wish, at this point, to switch to some other reading material to avoid distress.)

He pointed out that each of us has millions of ancestors and that, at conception, your sex is determined randomly. If any single one of that galaxy of ancestors had chanced to have a different sex, you would not be here to read this. (Presumably, someone else would. Unless of course one of *my* millions of ancestors met with a mishap.)

Keep that word "galaxy" in mind.

Just how many of your forebears were there that the wrong-gender accident could have happened to, thereby snuffing any chance of your existence? Brace yourself.

Alvarez led us gently to the wowing fact: An imaginary spaceship travels through our galaxy. Each of the millions of heavenly bodies in our galaxy represents one ancestor. But it gets better. (Or worse.)

The ship leaves our galaxy and journeys through the next. And the next.

And

Even typing this next bit makes me glad I'm sitting down. Not only does each planet, star, Milky Way, and what-have-you in every galaxy represent numerically a member of your family tree, so does *each atom* in all those galaxies. Every one representing a chance for each of us not to exist.

Had any one of those parents died before maturing, or been sterile, or not met the wife by chance in handing her a dropped glove, or shared a woolly mammoth bone with her on a date leading to bed, or been carried off in the plague or killed by some forerunner of a New York bicycle rider on the sidewalk . . . the mind boggles. (Not to mention the near-infinite number of people who might have been born down through the end of time but weren't—because your particular chain went on unbroken.)

Can any mind this side of Einstein's accommodate this thought?

How many ancestors, going back millions and millions of years—each of whose specific wiggly was in each case the only one among millions that got through to make you . . . how many of those ancestors are there?

Help me, math guys and gals. What's the answer? What to the tenth power?

There's more good stuff on this.

But for now, I have to lie down.

SEPTEMBER 10, 2010

Further Improbables

What good, smart reading your comments are on my column about how unlikely our existence is.

And all this having come about because of an enlightened Irving Junior High School (Lincoln, Nebraska) teacher's decision to risk her job by showing us in eighth grade a facts-of-life movie—instead of playing it safe with the Bible Belt parents by treating us to one of those less-than-stirring ERPI classroom films like *Hans and Helga Herd Their Sheep*. (How we giggled at "ERPI.")

The might-have and the might-not-have-beens in all this can flood your mind.

In thinking that you and I are one of Walter Alvarez's "astronomically improbables," it's only a small mental step to realizing who else, specifically, had to be, too.

Inevitably, Adolf Schicklgruber leaps to mind. (In fact, it was only his grandmother's name.) Had any one of millions of other egg-sperm combinations chanced to happen, a Hitler-free world would be, to put it mildly, a different place. (How dark a mind-set would you have to be burdened with to think *Yeah, and we could have gotten someone even worse?*)

Other names begin to crowd the head, in no particular order. Roosevelt. And Churchill. Tojo and Patton. Submit your own favorites to be grateful—or ungrateful—for.

Think of the world with or without (I'll type as they pop into my head): Jonas Salk, Orson Welles, Genghis Khan, Lincoln, Julia Ward Howe and her "Battle Hymn," Groucho Marx, Saint Joan, Mark

Twain, Frank Sinatra, Edith Wharton, the Mills Brothers, Mozart, Michelangelo, Brando, Jackie Robinson, Albert Einstein, Louis Armstrong, Laurel and Hardy, Stewart and Colbert, Garbo, John Lennon, R. M. Nixon, Bobby Fischer, the Modern Jazz Quartet, Picasso, Joe McCarthy, John Wayne, Charles Manson, Charles Dickens, Mohammed, Muhammad Ali, Plato, Edward Albee, Liz and / or Dick, Christopher Columbus.

Sarah Palin and Curly of the Three Stooges.

Not to mention the fathers of the atom bomb. (Were there mothers?) What if the atom were as yet unsplit? Think of it.

What if all of them had been canceled out by our random selection? What might a whole other comparable set have been?

Whoops. Can't help noticing I haven't put in that lad with no college education who nonetheless made his mark. The talented one from Stratford-upon-Avon.

And good heavens, so to speak: What of Jesus?

I can't help wondering how, if there were a magazine called *The Creationist's Monthly*, this astounding subject would be treated. My brilliant Old Testament teacher at Yale, the esteemed B. Davie Napier, said that Genesis can be read as a poetic expression by its author of God's creation of the world as akin to the potter's (loving) creation of his vase. A view that gets around the awkwardness of the seven days problem and the carbon dating—and those pesky fossils.

One commenter confessed to being knocked over by the incalculable odds against his existence but able to come to terms with the theological implications by deciding that it was God who chose his particular bit of sperm over the millions available. (A touch of ego here?)

Somewhere in the year after having seen the ERPI film, a troubling thought hit me: my conception took a single instant.

When you're a kid, your world is upended on that memorable day when you learn of That Thing Called Sex (possibly Cole Porter's original song title for the more socially acceptable "What Is This

Thing Called Love"?) and then you're jolted by the thought, "Could this mean this thing was done by—oh my God!—Mummy and Daddy? In bed?" (Let alone the preposterous thought of Grandma and Grandpa breathing hard.)

Then comes the whopping, forehead-smacking thought, which in my case was: "Does this mean that when Mom and Dad were, er, um, in the act of sexual congress . . ." (I doubt that I put it that way. As an adult, I much prefer the British "at it like knives." Let me start a new sentence.) What if, during the act that gave the world me— and you—the phone had rung in the middle of everything? Resumption on the parents' part later would have resulted in—not me, or you, but "not-me" and "not-you."

(I was thirteen and in the bathtub again—where thoughts seem to hit—when this one did; I recall that, for whatever reason, it made my legs involuntarily jump, causing a terrific splash. Can someone explain?)

Resumption on the parents' part would have meant an entirely different configuration of those eager little wigglers assaulting Mom's egg. Who, I wondered, would be in this tub now? Followed by the unsettling thought, "It might even be a *girl*."

Troubling thoughts swarmed. My best friend, Mary, could have been somebody else. And my favorite uncle, Paul. And Hopalong Cassidy. And the old sod who fondled my naughty bits in the movie theater. Every single person in my life could have been somebody else. Including, happily, Mrs. G., my sixth-grade teacher . . .

Now hear this lovely tale from Walter Alvarez's talk on this subject at the EG conference I mentioned last time. It bears the unfortunate trait of being true.

A man and his fiancée boarded a plane from New York to California. They had two tickets (of course) but only one was first class. The fellow, perhaps feeling he couldn't afford to be seen in coach with lesser folk, assumed the first-class seat. His mate-to-be sat in coach.

This random world had placed next to her a man. Midway

through the flight, her fiancé came back from first class to check on her and found her, and the man, laughing merrily. And cozily.

Can you guess the rest?

I wonder if she chose the moment of claiming their luggage to inform her until-that-moment fiancé that he would be spared the expense of a wedding ring. She had found her man.

In light of what we've been talking about, think what the one fellow's selfish act did to the possible children of his that might have issued, had he sprung for another first-class ticket. Or merely been a gentleman. And those probable children of the woman and her attractive seatmate.

And the broken chain of ancestry in the one case, and the probable new chain of descendants down through the ages.

Might the "new" chain produce a cancer curer? Or might the other have?

Whew!

SEPTEMBER 24, 2010

The Titan and the Pfc.

Eddie Fisher dead at eighty-two.

I was not much of a fan of Eddie Fisher's and his death didn't mean much to me, but he'd been on my mind thanks to the remarkably hard-to-put-down (in the physical sense) new book about Richard Burton and Elizabeth Taylor, *Furious Love*, by Sam Kashner and Nancy Schoenberger. And the punishing role Eddie played in their lives.

Something about his death rang a faint bell. But about what? I needed a memory hearing aid to detect the distant tone. Had I had him on a show and forgotten? (Anyone who's done five ninety-minute shows a week for even one year can tell you that that can happen. As when you bump into a celebrity and say, "I'm sorry we never did a show together"—and his face falls, and . . . it's too awful to think about.)

Then, suddenly, with nothing apparent triggering it, the answer appeared. The name George S. Kaufman glimpsed in a bookstore window did it.

It was one of my favorite early-days-of-television memories and I had written about it once in an introduction to a book called *By George*, a collection of the great playwright, director, and Algonquin wit's writings and sayings. I can't find the book and I can't forget the story.

Groucho always referred to Kaufman as "my personal god."

In the years I was lucky enough to know Groucho, there was one trait of the elderly that I, at least, never experienced in him. The one where you have to pretend to be hearing an oft-told joke or story for the first—rather than the seventh or eighth—time.

With one exception. Kaufman had known and written for the Brothers Marx—the original Fab Four (then three)—and Groucho worshipped him.

It went: "Did I ever tell you the greatest compliment I ever got?"

I said no the first time and also the four or five times thereafter over the years. I can hear Groucho's familiar soft voice in my mind's ear: "The greatest compliment I ever got was from George S. Kaufman." I expected a joke.

"George said to me once, 'Groucho, you're the only actor I'd ever allow to ad-lib in something I wrote.' And that's the greatest compliment I ever got." (Each time, he teared slightly.)

I loved hearing this treasured story repeated. It was no trouble pretending to hear it for the first time.

And now to our story.

Kaufman was one of three panelists on a live black-and-white TV show called *This Is Show Business*. A performer would come on, tell the panel a problem of his, perform, and then return to sit before the panel. Each panelist would then comment on the person's "problem." (There is a tantalizing glimpse of the great man on this show, on YouTube.)

On the memorable night, Pfc. Eddie Fisher—in uniform, looking about sixteen—laid out his problem. It was a complaint. He said he was appearing at the Copacabana nightclub and because of his extreme youth and boyish looks, none of the gorgeous showgirls would consent to go out with him. Then he sang, probably, "O Mein Papa" and sat down to receive the panel's remarks and advice.

It began with "the Gloomy Dean of American Comedy," as Kaufman had been labeled by someone. (My guess would be the wit Oscar Levant.) Kaufman's dark countenance as he balefully gazed upon the juvenile Mr. Fisher promised something good—but what? Though I'm working from memory, the thing is so indelible in my mind that I can just about guarantee you that what follows is no more than—here and there—a few words off. At a measured pace, Kaufman began:

"Mr. Fisher, on Mount Wilson there is a telescope. A powerful telescope that has made it possible to magnify the distant stars to approximately twelve times the magnification of any previous telescope.

(*Pause.*)

"And, Mr. Fisher, atop Mount Palomar sits a more recently perfected telescope. This magnificent optical instrument can magnify the stars up to six times the magnification of the Mount Wilson telescope."

(*Where is he going?* I wondered, glued to the screen, back in Nebraska.)

He went on:

"As improbable as it would doubtless be, if you could somehow contrive to place the Mount Wilson telescope inside the Mount Palomar telescope, Mr. Fisher . . . you still wouldn't be able to see my interest in your problem."

(*Pandemonium.*)

The laugh seemed to go on long enough for me to go make a sandwich and come back before it had stopped.

I never met the man. At about age eighteen, I did once see Kaufman plain—with the trademark high-piled black hair—enter a Broadway theater on an opening night, with a beautiful lady on his arm.

A dear friend, the actress Leueen MacGrath—then a former but still devoted Mrs. George Kaufman—used to unwittingly torture me by saying, "George would have enjoyed you so." It gets to me, just typing it.

Leueen said that, seemingly aloof, he was softhearted and sentimental beneath the forbidding exterior. He is known to have personally financed, quietly and anonymously, the escape of many Jews from Hitler's Germany.

I still regret not having bought—years ago and short on

funds—from a New York autograph dealer a single sheet of notepaper from the Ritz Hotel in Boston. Kaufman would have been directing a Broadway-bound play there. In jet black and boldly inscribed with a broad-nibbed pen, it read:

> The Ritz, Boston
> I don't want any German plays.
> Geo. S. Kaufman

A young generation, conspicuously ignorant of everything before the day of their birth, would know nothing of this great wit, prolific playwright, and director. (I'd love to teach a course called "Kaufman, Benchley, Thurber, Perelman, Parker, Lardner, and, of the Numerous Comic Allens, Fred, and Others You Were Too Dumb to Have Been Born in the Time of, 101.")

Who can fail to love a man who could suddenly pun in the middle of a poker game, "One man's Mede is another man's Persian."

Who was stopped at the stage door of a play he was directing by a new doorman who challenged, "Are you with the show?" Kaufman: "Let's just say I'm not against it."

Who could tell a shifting and fidgeting stage actor, "Don't just do something; stand there."

Who could say to a woman endlessly chattering at a dinner table, "Do you have any unexpressed thoughts?"

I should include here a story Groucho liked to repeat. It was his favorite about Kaufman. It is fairly well known, but I hate to think there's anyone who hasn't heard it.

(This story as well as one or two more of these have occasionally been attributed to others, but who wouldn't want to claim them? Groucho's word is good enough for me.)

Alfred Bloomingdale—of New York's great department store—decided to dabble in the world of theater and produce a Broadway play. One of Kaufman's great talents was as a "play doctor," and with his revising and rewriting and editing skills, he was renowned for turning more than one person's potential turkey into a play with a chance.

Bloomingdale's play was—in the nightmare phrase—"in trouble out of town." At such times, the cry was "Get Kaufman!"

Bloomingdale transported Kaufman in limousined style to the Shubert Theater in New Haven, where his play was "trying out." When the curtain came down, Kaufman was seen heading for the car to go home to New York. Observers reported the following:

Bloomingdale bustled over, blocked Kaufman's way, and breathlessly confronted him with "Well, George, you've seen my show. Please, tell me! I've put an awful lot of money into this show. What should I do?"

Kaufman: "Close the show and keep the store open nights."

That night, in that New York theater lobby so many years ago, when I only *saw* him, couldn't I have at least walked over and said hello?

OCTOBER 8, 2010

Match Him? Not Likely

He was devilishly fun to be around.

Whatever his dark side may have been, in the times we spent together I saw only the effervescence. Bernie Schwartz appeared to be having the time of his life being Tony Curtis.

I suppose I say "appeared" because despite the exuberance, his life was not unadulterated bliss, and the marital sort terminated five times. The sixth marriage lasted. He said once, "I wouldn't be caught dead marrying a woman young enough to be my wife."

He was a man who admitted that his one driving early ambition in life was simply to be a movie star, and he managed to achieve that (some would say) shallow goal.

But he did more. He went on to become not just a dapper guy for whose looks women tumbled in droves. He also proved he was more than only—in one of several phrases that plagued him—a "pretty boy" of the screen. He became a fine realistic film actor.

(Any doubts? See *Sweet Smell of Success*. Or, if that's not enough, *The Defiant Ones*.)

Before he managed to moderate his marked Bronx accent, he was stuck with a line uttered in an early costume drama in which he allegedly committed, "Yonda lies da castle of my fodda."

He was sensitive about it. When I asked him about that, Tony declared it a bum rap. He blamed Debbie Reynolds for popularizing it by inventing and spouting it on a talk show and in a context he also took to be shaded with "maybe a little anti-Semitism" when she included the words, "Tony Curtis isn't his real name."

I asked him if in fact he ever said it. He said he didn't, but confessed to a similar line. It was in the negligible film *Son of Ali Baba*. I wish I knew the line he admitted to. Could it have contained the words "valley of the stream" or some such? Perhaps a costume drama idiot savant reading this can supply the answer? It's early as I type this, and I hate to awaken Robert Osborne.

In a memoir called *American Prince*, he complained of often being made to feel like a second-class citizen in movieland, receiving haughty snubs from the likes of, among others, Reynolds, Ray Milland, and Henry Fonda. This apparently made him feel like a slum kid at the prom.

He and I did a memorable magic act on my ABC show. I lay on a low table, Tony dramatically made incantations and sorcerish gestures, and I slowly floated upward a few feet. He passed a solid hoop over me and I descended. The audience was stunned.

As an International Brotherhood of Magicians card carrier, I can't reveal the details; but what I am about to say will be understood by magicians. Owing to hasty rehearsal and, um, slightly erroneous head placement on my part, not only did I levitate but so did, separate from me, a small piece of the table. To the layman, perhaps puzzled by the small fragment of gravity-defying lumber accompanying my rise, nothing was thereby revealed. (Cross my heart there were no wires.)

On an earlier show I told Tony that among magicians, at least some of them forgave him for the dreadful, phony film *Houdini*. He laughed.

He made a big public show of quitting smoking, and came on the show distributing buttonhole pins with "I.Q." for ("I Quit") on them. Whether or not cocaine replaced nicotine, I don't know, but an actor friend of mine, more staid than Mr. Curtis, was appalled at Tony's apparently openly snorting magic nose powder on the set between takes in, as I recall, the 1970s.

On another show, Tony took questions directly from the studio audience. Considering that we taped "to time" and did no editing, it took a certain amount of guts to take unrestricted questions this way, but Tony was willing to do it. I'd have liked to do this on my show more often, but there were few takers. For those fearless ones, it was not only fun, but obviously you got more credit for a line born on the spot.

Allen (Woody) had no fear of this. Once a female audience member, apparently egged on by her school chums, yelled out, "Woody, do you think sex is dirty?"

Allen: "It is if you do it right."

Perhaps on that same show, a question from a complaining out-of-towner ended with "What makes New York so crummy?"

D.C.: "Tourists."

A funny, funny story about Tony has come down in more than one version. Here is how it reached my ears from one of the two principals, the great Walter Matthau.

Bernie Schwartz, poor kid from—to say the least—humble beginnings, had only recently morphed into Tony Curtis. His friend Matthau was still in the New York theater and Tony had just done a couple of bits in movies.

Walter came out of Sardi's, "the actors' restaurant" on West Forty-Fourth Street, from lunch. It was a Wednesday afternoon and the area was populated with both white- and blue-haired matinee ladies.

Amidst a group of them, across the street, stood one man.

Matthau said that suddenly his name was being shouted. Above the sounds of traffic, he heard:

"Walta! Hey, *Walta*! Over *here*! It's me, Bernie! I just—"

I'm afraid that certain restrictions, understandable (mostly to others), apply here that render me unable to complete this anecdote in its original verbiage. But let's just say it involved Yvonne De Carlo.

In pace requiescat.

OCTOBER 22, 2010

I Wrote It, Must I Also Hustle It?

There is a price to be paid when your book comes out.

You have to go out and sell it.

I just did twelve—or was it fourteen?—back-to-back radio interviews from New York to Seattle and, so it seemed after five of them, all points in between.

Somewhere around number eight you begin to lapse into a kind of dream state, wondering if what you just said was something you had said to the same person ten minutes ago; or was that said to the previous host? Maybe he is the one you said it twice to? Or do you think you just said it now but in fact only *thought* it?

You want to go back to bed.

Not every aspect of the thing is that bad, of course. It's fun for me to go on other folks' talk shows. When you've endured the ups and downs and tensions and pitfalls of hosting, being a guest is a piece of angel food.

And should it go badly, it's not your show.

And you must remind yourself that television sells books. In my day, I made a goodly number of overnight bestsellers of other people's books. It's a sort of scary experience in a way, partly because you can't help thinking how many deserving books might have achieved bestsellerdom if they'd gotten the chance.

In many worthy cases the TV boost helped overcome the notorious skills of publishers at killing book sales for the author.

A favorite publishing technique for ruining years of hard work is to fumble getting the book into stores until after its limited "shelf life" has expired and it's all too late—and the maddened author wishes to assemble a Molotov cocktail and . . .

(Should the idea of a major publishing house seemingly forgetting to put a book in bookstores until too late seem far-fetched, there's a way you can verify this: ask anybody.)

Way back I learned that some enterprising entrepreneurs were offering a service teaching how to plug your book on TV. I had on my show one of their graduates, apparently, who had gone a little overboard on one piece of advice. See if you can guess what it was:

> Mr. Cavett, when I conceived of my book *Misadventure* [let's call it] I thought, I want *Misadventure* to be different. I want people to say, I bought *Misadventure* because *Misadventure* sounds like the kind of book . . . etc.

Have you guessed? Somewhere near the dozenth chiming of the title, the audience began to make a sort of audible wince. I let it go and moved on to one more guest, but in thanking the guests and bringing the show to a close I allowed myself a minor pleasure. I thanked the author and added, "Did I give you a chance to mention the title of your book?"

The burst of laughter seasoned with scattered applause caused me momentary guilt. It soon passed.

In turning a collection of earlier columns into a book it was necessary to read through them all again, something I might never otherwise have done. I'm glad it happened, because there were quite a few surprises. I'm almost afraid to ask other writers if they, too, have found themselves surprised when doing this at how many things were themselves surprises. The first time you come across a passage that is as new to you as if its author were someone else, it's a bit unsettling. "I don't remember having that thought" is, well, a strange thought.

On the other side of the coin, there are the ones that make you cringe, seeing them now, as you realize what a much better wording would have been.

Faithful readers may forgive me here for repeating that invaluable quote from Mark Twain: "The difference between the almost right word and the right word is the difference between the lightning bug and the lightning."

The delightful side of the coin (we're dealing with a multisided coin here) is the passage that makes you howl with laughter, again with that sense of seeing it for the first time and wondering who could have written it.

I don't feel guilty confessing to howling at my own humor, having once asked the great S. J. Perelman if he ever did so upon rereading himself.

"Heavens to Betsy, yes," said that genius, lapidary wordsmith. "Sometimes I find myself re-perusing a paragraph from former times and rolling over and over on the floor with laughter, marveling at the intricacy of the mind that wrought such gems."

Before getting ready for the next plugola session, let me toss in a special item.

Gratified at how many loved the Kaufman / Fisher column, I here offer again, all too briefly, the great playwright and director (and Groucho's personal god) George S. Kaufman.

Again, the setting is that same variety / panel show *This Is Show Business*.

A rather aggressive borscht circuit comic, vastly contrasting in style from G.S.K., came on the show to perform and plug his new book. Ill-advisedly, while facing the panel, he decided to match wits with the master. Let's call the boisterous comic "Danny."

Danny: So how'd you like my book, Mr. Kaufman?
Kaufman: I enjoyed it very much.
Danny: No kiddin'. Who read it to you?
Kaufman: The same person who wrote it for you.

NOVEMBER 12, 2010

Lennon's Return

When I entered their room, bed is where the Lennons were. I'm afraid that that sentence seems to promise more than will be delivered. Let's come back to it.

The buzz was all over town. The Lennons—yes, those two—had agreed to come on the Cavett show.

In truth, they had all but fully agreed to. As a condition, they'd asked that we meet before they said a final yes; presumably as a test for possible incompatibility. There proved to be, mercifully, anything but.

Had they not done the show I would have been sorry, of course, to miss enjoying the envy of all the shows that didn't get them first. Or at all.

Yoko was sweet and cordial, and John and I got on instantly. He was too complex a man to be described in a few adjectives, but one of them would have to be "accessible." He was easy and comfortable immediately, and I'm sorry I can only recall a single example of the sort of relaxed banter we exchanged from the start.

He said, "I guess the reason we feel we'd like to do this is that you have the only halfway intelligent talk show on television."

"Are you sure you want to be on a show that's halfway intelligent?" I ventured.

John laughed. Then he put me in a movie.

I stood against a wall with several other people and we simulated passing a whispered joke from right to left. I'm not sure what

the joke was, but I'm told it did end up in the film. No other immediate movie offers poured in.

John said that just before I got there they had filmed a
dream sequence there in the hotel room in which Yoko imagines
she is dancing with Fred Astaire. Yoko played herself and the male
part was played by Fred Astaire. (They had run into him in the
lobby.)

Now, about that bed. They were not so much in bed as on bed.
This was at the St. Regis Hotel.

It was such a vast specimen that I wondered if they had had it
specially constructed to be bigger than king-sized. (Kingdom-sized?)
Its half acre of surface seemed to serve as their work area. Various
notebooks and papers and odd objects and drawing pads and projects
populated its surface. There must have been another bed somewhere
in the regal suite for mere sleeping.

They did the show. Twice, in fact. The first show was a smash, getting better as it went along. They were nervous at first, evidenced
by their killing half a pack of Viceroys between them in the first few
segments, settling down gradually into what proved a delightful and
increasingly smoke-free ninety minutes.

Later, I ended up testifying on John's behalf when the Nixon
White House was trying to have him deported.

But I didn't see much of the Lennons between those shows and
John's awful death.

John and I exchanged a few letters, his in an entertaining and
distinctly Joycean style. I tried to find them for a quote here. My
optimistic view is that I have only misplaced them.

Had I lived where I do now I might have heard the fatal shots. I
asked someone who was there to remind me: Did John know he had
been shot? A policeman, I'm told, in the race to the hospital, asked
John if he was aware what was happening and did he know who he
was. He did.

I recall getting a good bit of hate mail for a remark I made at the

time about the gun lobby and how democratic they were in including the mentally ill among those with easy access to firearms.

I just watched one of those shows on DVD. In a moment I'd
forgotten, John is lightheartedly contemplating old age. "Some day
we'll be an old couple living on the south coast of Ireland, saying
[feeble old codger voice] 'I remember when we were on *The Dick
Cavett Show.*'"

It wasn't poignant at the time.

DECEMBER 10, 2010

A Bittersweet Christmas Story

Snow was predicted for Lincoln, and there was every reason to think it would be a really fine Christmas.

Having recently received the remarkable gift of puberty with its attendant wonders, I had my hopes up for another great present, not exactly comparable: a longed-for piece of magical apparatus I had reason to believe would be under the tree on Christmas Eve.

We always opened packages then instead of on Christmas Day, and in a sort of Norman Rockwellian tableau: nice warm house, a Nebraska snowfall settling outside, and relatives of varying ages and beloved Sandy, my big, manly spaniel, all semicircled around the gifts arrayed under the tree.

It's sad to think how cozy such Midwestern family Christmases were when you were that age, and how odiously I now view the allegedly jolly season, with its trampling crowds and extorted gifts. But let that pass.

Back then, in that far-off happier time, Christmas was magical when it finally arrived with excruciating slowness.

Nobody, when you're that age, could ever convince you that there would come a day when all those chatty, friendly uncles, aunts, parents, and grandparents in that comfy circle, contentedly digesting dinner around the tree, would be . . . gone. That you yourself would someday be the sole surviving link in that warm family circle. Unthinkable.

Without even shutting my eyes I can summon an aural montage of the pleasant chatter and those unvarying phrases used every year: the "Oh, how beautifuls" and "Oh, you shouldn't haves" and "Where on earth did you find its?" The sometimes mendacious "How did you know I wanted one?" and the well-worn "It's a shame to spoil the wrapping." (I could never see why.)

Every one of those Christmas Eves is interchangeable and identical in memory, and they usually ended with "Well, we'd better be getting home before the snow gets any deeper" and the hugs and kisses goodnight and confessions of having eaten too much.

All interchangeable, that is, except for one.

My step-grandparents lived next door. The father of my college-professor, former-Marine-captain stepmother was known by his first initials, T.R., and was a book salesman for Scott, Foresman, the publisher who gave us Dick and Jane. He sired six offspring, three of each.

He was a huge and imposing man and I always thought he looked just like a local statue of William Jennings Bryan. He had a voice so deep it made Orson Welles sound like Truman Capote. When booming "You big bum!" at referees at Nebraska football games, it caused everybody in the stadium who wasn't deaf to jump, turn around, and look.

On this particular Christmas Eve, T.R. seemed uncharacteristically nervous. My beloved Aunt Harriet had assumed the job of picking up presents from under the tree and handing them to the recipients. After a while T.R., exuding growing anxiety, urged her to "take some from this side of the tree." "Hold your horses," said Harriet, being a daughter of some independence.

His agitation increased. "Give Mom one" only produced, from Harriet, further refusal to be directed.

T.R.'s agitation and uneasiness began to assume health-issue proportions. I worried that we were going to have a Christmas remembered for T.R.'s clutching his chest, pitching forward, and expiring among the gifts and Christmas frippery.

A couple more "Give Mom ones" finally became an exasperated "Give Mom that little blue package right there." Harriet relented. It was given.

What happened next is remembered almost as something out of fiction. Like something that happens in a certain kind of harmless-seeming short story that contains a jolt.

Bertha—an overweight yet handsome woman—unwrapped what it became instantly clear was a jewelry box. T.R. hovered nearby, breathing audibly in anticipation.

She flipped open the lid, revealing a ring with a good-sized diamond that shot sparks into the room.

Without removing the ring—and while emitting a sort of low growl—with a backhand swing of the arm, she flung box and ring away. The innocent box and contents flew about six feet, smacked the wall, and bounced to the floor.

She spat out, "That doesn't make up!"

The whole scene seemed to freeze-frame into a still picture. T.R. began to cry and tried to put a hand on her shoulder. It, too, was flung away. I didn't know where to look.

Somehow the evening ended.

How does memory edit such happenings? The moment was so vivid that I have no recall of the next, inevitable attempted comfortings and awkward departures. Did we open the rest of the presents in the poisoned atmosphere? Probably someone with aplomb suggested we were all tired and should finish Christmas on Christmas Day.

It seems as if days went by before I had whatever minimal courage it took to ask my stepmother about the shocking thing.

"Mom had a pretty tough time with Dad," she said. "Living in little western Nebraska towns. He was the principal at Chadron, not making much. He was gone a lot. Mom had wanted to teach school. She was quickly saddled with kids, starting with me. The last thing in the world I think Mom wanted was the six of us. Two, maybe. Mom was an intelligent woman and felt that a woman's life should consist of something more than pushing the next generation around in baby carriages. Being the oldest, I had to take care of the two youngest because by then Mom had simply had it with motherhood."

I'd gotten old enough to be able to ask why she had to have so many kids. Did she, um, not know what was causing them?

"That's not the sort of thing you spoke to your mother about then, but I wondered, too. I shouldn't say this, but I sometimes think Dad insisted. I hate to think it, but maybe he even—how can I put this?—forced himself on her."

All this was a bit over my head. My image of these two kindly old folks living next door on our elm-lined street—I thought contentedly—was now murky. Did everybody I thought liked each other not like each other? And why had the accumulated rage come out just then? In front of everybody? For maximum embarrassing revenge?

How many other people in my world were not what they seemed? It's safe to say that the moment that ring hit the wall, my notion of the adult world altered. There must be a lot of things in it I didn't understand.

The incident submerged from memory until, home from college years later, I found an old album with a picture of a young, handsome, and smiling couple on a long-ago wedding day, beaming before the camera. They were the (youthful) purchaser and rejecter of the Christmas ring. It brought to mind those pictures in the paper of a grinning couple or family, taken before one of them committed murder.

I know it sounds a bit contrived, but on that same trip, if not the same day, brushing up on some assigned Congreve, I came across the eternally misquoted couplet that ends with "Nor Hell a fury like a woman scorn'd."

But it's the preceding line that brought that grinning young couple in the old wedding photo—T.R. and Bertha—to mind: "Heav'n has no Rage, like Love to Hatred turn'd."

Especially on Christmas Eve.

DECEMBER 24, 2010

Sauce for the Goose? Take a Gander

To this day I don't know what made me do it.

But if it's possible to get drunker than I got that night I can't imagine it.

It was not a party, celebration, New Year's Eve, or a wedding night; mine or anyone else's.

I blame Jerry Lewis.

I met Jerry when he hosted *The Tonight Show* for a fortnight in 1962 during the interim weeks between Jack Paar's exit and Johnny Carson's taking over. I found him to be an intelligent and personable man; more of both than I might have guessed.

In the next year, ABC gave Jerry an unprecedented, history-making two hours live on Saturday night. He remembered me and, apparently, my writing, and I joined his staff in Hollywood. Our continued friendship may have been partly rooted in his paying me four times more than I had ever made before.

Before I got the job, and still out of work, I stood frozen in my manager's office as I heard him negotiating the deal. "I'm sorry, but my client does not work for a thousand dollars a week."

Just as he was about to hang up in true tough-nosed negotiating style I wanted to yell, "That's right. He works for $360 a week!"

It got settled and I got the job. The much-heralded project was launched with a gala opening night, lavish even by Hollywood standards—complete with searchlights—at the old El Capitan Theatre (briefly renamed the Jerry Lewis Theatre), near legendary Hollywood and Vine.

Jerry, in a true Lewisian gesture, made the gala opening night special in a way I've never heard of before or since. He dressed himself and all the guests in tuxedos. But not only the guests. Camera operators, stage hands, ushers, off-camera crew, men invisible up in the flies wore, many for the first time, no doubt, black tie. A nervy youth (at twenty-six), I asked him why. "You dress a man's talent," he said.

Gowns dressed the handful of ladies' talents.

Even the traditional opening-night gift baskets were extra-lavish. Each included a fifth of Johnnie Walker Black Label. (Note this for later.)

My little apartment in the Bel-Air Arms—technically in Bel-Air, but up against the freeway and so far from the swanky, mansioned part of Bel-Air that it might as well have been in Kansas—was the typical two-story rectangular affair surrounding the inevitable swimming pool. Apartment #1 housed the inevitable cranky landlady.

The big night came and went. The critics were not kind, and with a numbing unanimity. The first show got reviews comparable to the account of the attempted mooring of the Hindenburg at Lakehurst.

Although the show got much better—and some of them were terrific—it never really recovered from that awful night. And then Kennedy was assassinated, casting a pall on everything, and after a few more weeks at a loss that would run a small nation for a year, ABC pulled the plug.

As we slumped through the remaining few weeks, just about everyone was depressed.

My enjoyment of the silliness of Hollywood had faded. I'd seen the La Brea Tar Pits, so what was left? I had no love life to speak of, or even think of, and decided I had to do something I'd never done. But what?

My opening-night Johnnie Walker bottle, still virginal, was by then the only survivor of the gift basket. I'd been using it to replace a missing bookend. How about seeing what the fun is in getting really drunk?

There was no maid at the Arms, and all the dishes and glasses were dirty. But there was a water cooler with those little paper cups. I filled one and embarked on my adventure.

I downed it in a series of short, prissy little gulps. I felt something. "Am I now really drunk?" I thought, probably aloud. I derived a sort of satisfying sense of manliness from not resorting to water, soda, 7-Up, Pepsi, or whatever it was you drank scotch with.

"No, thanks. I take it straight," I said to no one.

Up to that time I had had drinks, of course. But one and rarely two were always more than enough to disturb my equilibrium.

Strange things began to happen. I had decided to be lavish and fill a new cup for each new portion of firewater. Since I was sure I was on only my third one, why were there six or seven empties now on the coffee table? And why was the bottle suddenly more than half empty? Had I spilled some?

By now I had started pretending the paper cups were glasses, hurling them into an imaginary fireplace with a hearty "Long live the king!" Then, "Hey, why don't we take ourselves a little walk in the balmy California night air?" (I was now openly talking aloud. And the voice wasn't entirely familiar.)

I had the crazy thought, "What's good enough for the Scott Fitzgeralds at the Plaza fountain is good enough for me. Let's jump into the pool fully clothed." I agreed with this thought.

I was on the second floor and the steps down to the pool seemed unfamiliarly rubbery, sort of like walking on a trampoline. Balancing with a bit of trouble on the edge of the deep end of the pool, I decided I should take off my good shoes—but then vetoed this on the grounds that it would compromise my flamboyant and daring stunt, which had now assumed in my mind glamorous and heroic proportions.

But then, a touch of compromise. I congratulated myself on having one sensible thought. My Bulova wristwatch from high school graduation was not waterproof. I took it off, placed it in my pocket, and jumped in. I kept its pitiful corpse for years.

The moment my fully clad body cannonballed (hoping to awaken the crabby landlady) into the aqua and rotated eerily underwater, I shot out and up to my room, not really wanting to encounter the Medusa of Apartment #1, partly for fear of being kicked out if she identified the no-night-swimming-rule-breaking culprit; not thinking that it wouldn't have taken the talents of the famous resident of 221B Baker Street, London, to follow the dripped trail to my door.

I flopped onto the bed after what seemed like half an hour of peeling off sopping, tangling garments. Losing my balance a few times, I devised a sort of joke. I wondered, wobbling and reeling as I was, would a chance earthquake make me steady?

I'd felt the aftereffects of a couple of drinks before, but nothing close to what Ernie Hemingway so vividly described as having to keep your eyes open to stop the room from spinning.

The term "hangover" was still merely a word to me. I'd witnessed a ferocious one my freshman year. A fellow Yalie was tottering along the sidewalk, hoping to catch a late breakfast and looking twenty years older than he had the day before. He'd awakened after a fraternity binge with a hangover so bad he thought he was dying. "I felt so awful I wasn't sure I'd live," he told me, and then added, "I actually read the Bible."

Supine on the bed, gazing heavenward, I foolishly shut my eyes. The room rotated like an overhead fan. Nausea followed. Then sleep. But the full price of this goofy jape was as yet unpaid.

(Aftermath—maybe—to come. Too painful to contemplate right now.)

JANUARY 7, 2011

The Wrath of Grapes

And now, back to our story.

We left our hero self-victimized by the foolish notion that it might be fun to down somewhat more than half a bottle of scotch.

The price the next morning, should you never have learned so firsthand, is prodigious.

Struggling into a seated position on the edge of the bed, I gave the room a moment to settle down. It took a while to decide where I was. It took even longer to decide who.

The mouth was a distinct displeasure. I remember saying aloud, to no one, "It tastes like I've eaten an assortment of larvae." I tried to laugh but the head pain forbade any more than a murmur of self-appreciation. I made it to the sink as Vesuvius erupted.

Writers and actors have always been reliable sources of income for the alcohol industry, with some notorious examples: Barrymore, Fields, Burton, O'Toole, Faulkner, Robards, Bogart, Hemingway, and Fitzgerald, to name a fraction.

W. C. Fields once recalled that "we lost our corkscrew and had to live on food and water for several days." Of course, W.C. was a disciplined alcoholic, swearing "I never drink anything stronger than gin before breakfast."

Samuel Johnson's "This is one of the disadvantages of wine: it makes a man mistake words for thought" is akin to *Othello*'s "O God, that men should put an enemy in their mouths to steal away their brains!"

Lady Astor claimed she didn't drink because "I want to know when I'm having a good time."

The great Kingsley Amis, author of my favorite comic novel, *Lucky Jim*, and world-class consumer of both hard and only relatively milder stuff, came to mind earlier when I mentioned morning-after mouth. He has left us perhaps as close to the last word as we may ever get regarding the hangover:

> Dixon was alive again. Consciousness was upon him before he could get out of the way; not for him the slow, gracious wandering from the halls of sleep, but a summary, forcible ejection. He lay sprawled, too wicked to move, spewed up like a broken spider-crab on the tarry shingle of morning. The light did him harm, but not as much as looking at things did; he resolved, having done it once, never to move his eyeballs again. A dusty thudding in his head made the scene before him beat like a pulse. His mouth had been used as a latrine by some small creature of the night, and then as its mausoleum. During the night, too, he'd somehow been on a cross-country run and then been expertly beaten up by secret police. He felt bad.

Robert Benchley wrote often of his hangovers—the only cure for which he said was death—and which he detested almost as much as the pigeons that always "came rumbling in and out of my window."

"Best thing you can do is eat a big breakfast" began to sound in my head, along with other soundings there. Struggling into drier clothing than the soggy garments I had somehow gotten out of but slept among, following my watch-drowning ritual, I somehow drove in a painful (interior) haze a few blocks to the UCLA campus. I remembered a "Breakfast Is 'Our Specialty'" sign. The illiterate and unnecessary use of quotes for emphasis—as in DO NOT "LEAN" ON THE COUNTER—always amuses me, but it didn't then.

There, stepping gently because each footfall produced a sort of low timpani roll accompanied by a painful twinge in my head (I wondered if I had broken anything in there), I managed to arrange myself into a chair at a table for two, hoping to God no one would join me.

God apparently heard me.

Had anyone sat down, I wouldn't have been able to talk.

Giving the waitress my order caused the timpani to resume, and if anyone *had* sat down I decided I would scribble the words "deaf and dumb" on a napkin. "Laryngitis" would have done just as well, but I actually think it was less painful—and this sounds really silly—to think shorter words.

I had gotten out, sotto voce, the recommended voluminous breakfast: "Ham, eggs, toast, fried potatoes, coffee, and orange juice." The silly truth is that I had to recite the list twice. The first time, there had been no waitress standing there. Hallucination? When the real one appeared, I may have left off "please" because each syllable brought with it that nasty little twinge.

Almost magically, each bite seemed to contribute a measure of soothing.

Tottering less, I went next door to get a pair of sunglasses. I'd never known sunlight to be so punishing. They were expensive but I felt I couldn't really blame myself for not having thought of them back at the apartment. As it turned out, they went nicely with the pair I then found in my pocket. Nothing was going really well.

As I eased onto a park bench on the campus, the only positive thought I could come up with was that if I somehow lost one pair of sunglasses while sitting there, I had a backup.

I don't see much reason to go on further about this.

You are either one of the e-mailers from the first column who can too easily identify from experience, or one who can't, finding the whole thing tedious.

Did I learn anything from this folly?

Can't say I never imbibed again, but nothing even close to this nightmare.

I learned to wonder how in hell anyone can repeat such a self-torture throughout life. Surely the pain of the first bang-up hang-over becomes less as time goes by. Or doesn't it work that way? Wouldn't some sort of Pavlovian mechanism set in to keep you from sledge-hammering your own head on a regular basis? Pray tell.

I have no valuable advice to impart from my sodden and ill-advised Johnnie Walker experiment except for one thing.

Should you find yourself standing near me someday and should you for some reason utter the word "scotch" . . . stand back.

JANUARY 28, 2011

How Do You Open for a Mind-Reading Horse?

D o you, or someone else out there, have any idea what became of Ed Steib?

Let me make it easier. Maybe you remember him by the way he billed himself: "The Mysterious Mr. X and His Mind-Reading Horse."

I guess not.

It was one of those nice times of day on the prairies of Nebraska (Lincoln, in this case) when evening is setting in and the mourning doves begin their soft, three-note coo ("hoo, hoo, ho-*woo*-oo") that, wherever I hear it now, puts me right back on the glider on our front porch on Twenty-Third Street. (Are there still gliders?)

The phone rang. A sort of rough, rustic voice barked, "This is Ed Steib. Is this the young magician Dick Cavett I hear so much about?"

Since I was the only fourteen-year-old magician in Lincoln that I knew of with that name, I affirmed it.

"I want you to do a show with me and I'll pay you a hundred dollars."

As the old joke goes: I fainted and they brought me to. Then they brought me two more.

The vast sum mentioned was five times my highest fee to date.

One hundred smackers. And not to play Fairbury, or Broken Bow, or Beaver Crossing (yes), Nebraska, but Omaha! Omaha was to Lincoln, in my world, as New York is to Chicago. And a bright, impertinent young collegiate-type comic named Johnny Carson had a radio show from there.

When I told my dad, he wryly observed that one hundred dollars for one day's work was "not much. That's only one-eighth of what I made teaching school during the Depression—in a year!"

The show was to be in a big stadium and I could remember having marveled at Milton Berle there, playing to a sell-out crowd a year earlier. Now I was to be in those converging spotlights, cavorting like Uncle Miltie to an adoring sea of spectators.

Ed Steib said he had heard that I was good, adding that he had also heard that I was "a nice-looking kid." Could this have had anything to do with my dad's decision to accompany me on this gig? Also, there were no (legal) fourteen-year-old drivers in Nebraska.

I decided to feature my most stunning "effect" (magicians don't say "trick")—my rabbit vanish. A rabbit is placed in an ornate breakaway box, which is then dismantled, showing each piece on both sides. No rabbit.

The handmade (by me) Egyptian two-fold screen the box sat on is then placed aside. But a bit of white fur is visible. Feigning embarrassment I stand in front of it and try to go on despite raucous jeers and cries of "Turn it around!" When this reaches fever pitch, I do, revealing only the phrase "HA HA!"

My dad and I drove to Omaha the night before because there were two shows, the first an early matinee. This added to the excitement the need to spend a night in a hotel, back then still a glamorous adventure. I think it was the Hotel Rome. It brought to mind a hotel gag I used in my act: that they do change the sheets every day—from one room to another.

The momentous day dawned. Behind the stadium we were greeted by the affable Mr. X in person. You might cast him as a Nebraska farmer, probably of peasant German stock. Nearby grazed the Wonder Horse, looking decidedly untheatrical and a bit tired; probably, I figured, from the rigors of "the old two-a-day."

Outside the stadium were striking posters in black and red of Ed and his four-legged costar, with pictures apparently taken, in both cases, some years earlier.

I was steeped in the great language-gifted radio comedian Fred Allen back then and could turn him on in my head. (A harbinger perhaps of becoming a comedy writer?) I heard Fred saying, "Tell me, Mr. Steib, how long have you been wowing the populace with this spavined equine clairvoyant?"

The stage was a platform across from the grandstand.

I began setting up an hour before showtime to be sure to be ready when the crowd began to arrive. It was windy, and my dad got some tire chains out of our '38 DeSoto to anchor my aluminum magic table with its obligatory black felt top and gold fringe. Nearing showtime, the adrenaline started as I pictured the throngs pouring through the turnstiles and scrambling for seats.

And by showtime it was clear. Something had gone wrong.

Had the fair visitors missed all of the "Mr. X" posters tacked up along the busiest avenues of the fair? Or misread the time and date?

To put it at its breathtaking simplest, nobody showed up.

The clock ticked past showtime by a minute. Then two, three, four. And more. There was a dearth of customers, to the tune of none.

The vast interior seating area lacked a single living individual.

There was something awe-inducing about the sight of that stadium. For sheer, unadulterated emptiness I have never seen anything to match it.

I've seen empty rooms, empty closets, empty houses, empty theaters, and empty wheat fields. But for blank, unparalleled vacuity, nothing holds a candle to a yawning, empty stadium sleeping in the sun on a lazy summer afternoon in Nebraska. Pompeii when the ashes cooled was more populous than that grinning expanse of geometrically segmented concrete void.

I haven't been fully honest in this. There is something emptier: an empty stadium into which three people enter. A trio of would-be spectators were glimpsed for a moment, wandering in way up top, sitting down, looking around, and exiting.

Ed had a wonderful resilience. He shrugged the whole thing off as the result of poor placement of his "paper" (posters) and reminded me to be equally ready for the evening show. I'd forgotten about it.

The horse, too, appeared unfazed, but being psychic, had probably foreseen the whole thing.

My dad and I drove around Omaha and had lunch, and he tried to elevate my spirits by saying (A. B. Cavett being a humorist) that I was getting good experience at least in packing and unpacking my act. I was woeful and crestfallen but did my best not to let my father see it.

That night we packed them in.

By 8:00 the place was jammed with eager and noisy spectators.

I should mention that the majority may not have been Steib-and-Horse fans. For the night show, we were the intermission act to a stock car race. Obviously the addition of the race was just what the public needed to remind them of their eagerness to see Ed and me and the nag.

The only hitch was that the management, fearing running overtime, decided to dispense with the kid and his conjuring trumpery.

A bitter blow. God, how I wanted to play to that huge crowd.

Gloom abated considerably when Ed suddenly recalled that he needed an announcer; someone to read over the sound system the narration of his and his hairy partner's wonder show.

It seemed glamorous sitting up in the booth with the track announcer, reading from the faded, much-handled pages Ed gave me. I thrilled at hearing my voice boom out over the loudspeakers, making sure everyone saw that the blindfolded horse was stomping out the number of fingers held up by his master.

The only other showstopper I recall from the horse's repertoire was walking, blindfolded, up a seesaw or teeter-totter, tipping it, and proceeding down the other side, while in dramatic tones I pointed out that this would be difficult even for an un-blindfolded horse. (I couldn't tell if it occurred to the crowd, as it did to me, that even a horse wouldn't be dumb enough to try it un-blindfolded.)

Afterward, I was filled with the heady glow of having given a performance, if not exactly the one intended. There's nothing like a cheering crowd, I loved the "chills and spills" of the stock car race, and I was getting $100 to boot. Could Broadway be far off?

Halfway back to Lincoln it began to sink in that I hadn't done what I'd yearned to do: my act, cheered as Milton Berle had been by a huge crowd. No rabbit vanish.

Moreover, Ed hadn't so much paid me my $100 as told me he would, carefully noting down my address. And I had no reason to doubt his word. He had never not paid me before.

We were almost back to Lincoln when my father managed to include me in his vast amusement over the whole thing and we got to laughing so hard tears obscured the road. He advised me not to spend the money in one place, which set us off again.

But I wasn't yet suspicious or cynical enough to think my check might never appear.

"Aw, hell," my father said. "We had a thousand dollars' worth of fun out of it."

This was more than half a century ago. Have I become cynical, jaded, ungenerous, and hardened in the intervening years? I think not. Because when the money does come, I plan to give it to charity.

FEBRUARY 25, 2011

My Life as a Juvenile Delinquent

It was one of those delicious summer nights in Nebraska when you're blissfully wallowing in vacation. You gulp dinner in order to slip out through the screen door into the dark, into an atmosphere of rustling elm leaves and June bugs, and join up with some friends to play "kick the can" or "ditch" or to raise, if not hell, heck.

This night slipped over the line into the infernal.

My friend Tom Keene and a few more of us were out prowling. Neither Tom nor I can be certain who did what, or why. We were amusing ourselves fairly harmlessly, we thought, by picking up clods and small stones and tossing them noisily onto people's porches, then running when the porch light went on or someone looked out to see what was up.

At most, mischief.

Then somebody (me?) picked up a pop (soda, for easterners) bottle, or maybe it was a bigger rock. It's funny how, even though I'm not even sure I was the heaver, I can still see the missile arching toward the porch of what turned out be an elderly couple and smashing into the five- or six-foot etched-glass panel of their front door, reducing it—with a sickening crash—to a noisy cascade of glittering shards.

Not being totally stupid, we fled—in a phrase perhaps fairly new back in the fifties—like bats out of hell.

Apparently, we failed to run far enough. Someone had called John Law. Suddenly we were facing an approaching car that, as night prowlers, we knew (from the telltale extra-bright headlights) would be the fuzz. Soon we were inside it.

Using what may be some sort of police psychology, the two officers spoke no word. They just silently hauled our sorry little quartet to the station house.

Tom and I looked at each other as it struck us all at once that we were—holy mackerel!—in a *police station*.

It was, admittedly, somewhat romantic, but at the same time scary. Through an open door we could see a corner of an actual barred jail cell, just like in the movies.

Part of me wanted to be put in there for at least a while, to have a better story to tell, but most of me didn't. The words "bread and water" murmured ominously in my head. So did the sound of my dad reciting Wordsworth: "Shades of the prison-house begin to close / Upon the growing Boy."

Adding to the scariness was the fact that we were not quizzed as a group, but individually; undoubtedly the most effective technique. I don't recall having had a chance, once picked up by the cops, to conspire to lie. It apparently just came naturally. I remember one frightened voice whispering, "What if they hook us up to a lie detector?" They didn't.

Some primitive preservation instinct caused each of us, separately, to deny having done anything beyond being, unluckily, in the area where the crime had taken place. This seemed to have gone over well enough. But then something happened.

The third guy to go in for grilling—let's call him Barry, for indeed that was his name—threw a chill into the rest of us.

He emerged from his questioning crying. My guts gurgle even now, remembering the moment.

He didn't say he had ratted us out.

He didn't need to.

Then, another surprise. They let us go.

They were apparently smarter psychologists than we thought.

Or else quietly sadistic. Rather than saying that they now had the story and booking us, they released us to our consciences.

I slept horribly that night. The others reported the same.

When I read *Crime and Punishment* in later years, some of Raskolnikov's mental tortures rang all too familiar.

What would our parents do when they found out? Would we be kicked out of school? Put in that cell for real? With drunks and child gropers? The words "bread and water" played again.

My aching insomnia was so bad that night that I tiptoed to the medicine chest and dug out an unused pill I'd gotten from the dentist once for wisdom-tooth pain. It finally put me to sleep.

Nothing happened the next day, either. Tom said, "They're waiting for us to crack." A shrewd comment, as it happened.

It was now Saturday morning and I was on a local radio show produced by and for kids called *Storytime Playhouse*. I was able to lose myself in the fifteen-minute drama (as the director, I had awarded myself three choice roles, done in different voices) and totally forgot the whole thing. Until about three minutes after we went off the air.

I'd never experienced real gut-rending mental pain until then. We, the guilty gang, were beginning to look haggard. It was no longer mere speculation that Barry had shoved us overboard. With shame, he had admitted it, along with something about not being able to look his "mom in the eye." (You can imagine the scorn with which this wimpiness was greeted.)

Something had to be done. That something propelled me into the corner Walgreens phone booth a block from the radio station. I had half-formed a sort of scheme.

A bit of explanation: Even before puberty I had a low voice. "He sounds like a little man!" and other nauseating comments were always made around me. My postpubescent but still teenage vocal organ was that of an adult.

I became aware of this from time to time, as when I would ask a question of a public speaker from the back row. Everyone would turn around, dismissing diminutive me on sight as the source of the rumble.

Might this be our lifesaver? A force, unassociated with reason, drove me.

Although Walgreens was "air-cooled," I was sweating all over in my T-shirt and Lee jeans as I dialed the police station. The improbable dialogue that followed went something like this:

(*Phone picked up at station.*)

"Police headquarters, Collins speaking."

"Officer Collins, might you be the officer who questioned a group of fractious teenage boys the other night about a broken glass door?"

"Yes, that's right."

"Well, I have the dubious honor of being the father of one of those boys. And I must congratulate you, officer, on the masterful job you did handling this matter."

"Well, thank you. We try to do our best, of course."

"Well, I can assure you your psychology worked. Those poor kids have hardly slept since. And what they've done is take up a collection from their allowances and savings and put together a hefty envelope of cash, which they delivered to the old folks whose door glass they smashed. The people were damn nice about it and thanked and forgave them and even gave them something to eat." [*This, happily or unhappily, but certainly expensively, was true.*]

"Well, I'm glad to hear that. We usually wait a few days on a situation like this. One of the boys confessed and I hoped that it might eventuate [*cop-ese*] this way. I generally prefer to handle cases like this in that modality [*more cop-ese!*] rather than spoil the kids' 'record' with legal procedurism [*sic*]. I'm glad it seems to have culminated in a satisfactory resolution." [*My real father, an English teacher, might have advised the good officer on the desirability of using shorter words.*]

"Well, my hearty thanks to you, Officer Collins. You're a master psychologist and one hell of a policeman. Thanks again and good day to you, sir."

I hung up, as Woody Allen has said, sweating audibly.

In fact, I had waited just a moment or two to give the voice at the other end a chance to say, "Okay, you little bastard, how dumb do you think I am? Now you're really in trouble." And perhaps adding something about that dread phrase, "reform school."

Later, I seriously wondered what they might have charged me with. Impersonating a father?

I emerged from the booth in a mental state that combined both disbelief and a kind of foolish pride at the apparent success of my fourth acting role of the day. Then I went back in the booth and squandered another nickel, passing the good news to Tom to tell the other guys.

For a couple of days I had some doubts that this stunt had worked. But apparently it had. The sense of relief was indescribable. Guilt is not a desirable companion, and a particularly unpleasant bedfellow. The sky was open again.

It's unlikely that officer still lives and breathes. Something in me, over the years, wanted to call him and confess the whole charade. But I never did. I wish to hell I had.

Is it a bit hard for you to believe this youthful ruse, born of pain and desperation?

And what would an ethicist say?

MARCH 11, 2011

My Liz: The Fantasy

The setting is the Starlight Roof, or whatever it is or was called, at the top of what to me will always be "the RCA Building"; just as the MetLife Building remains "the Pan Am Building." (I resist all alterations to my adopted city.)

The scene is some sort of upscale fancy dinner party up there in the sky—sometime in the late eighties?—and I'm in the spotlight doing my trophy-winning rope routine from my old magic act, just as I've done it countless times since learning it from a master magician in my high school days. (Two-fifths of it could be seen for a while on YouTube, on Jimmy Fallon's show. The segment ran out of time and I owe Jimmy three-fifths of the classic "George Sands Rope Routine.")

Back to the party. At the point of completing one cut and restoration, I would toss the rope into the audience to lure the person who catches it up to the stage to do the rest of the cuttings, with me miraculously restoring the rope each time to astonished gasps and applause.

That night, about halfway back among the dimly lit diners, I'd glimpsed a female figure who, in the near-darkness, could almost have passed for Elizabeth Taylor, if you squinted.

In a merry jest, something made me say, "I've done this trick a hundred times and I keep having this fantasy that some day the person who comes up and helps me will be some famous, luminous movie star. Like Elizabeth Taylor."

Just before tossing the rope out front, I detected movement in the dark. I could see a striking apparition in white, gliding smoothly like a Rose Bowl float toward the floor-level stage.

It was.

And it was true what's been said so often. Her beauty would take your breath away.

(Better, I guess, than if her breath would take your beauty away.)

I'd love to know the technical explanation of a strange phenomenon. First gazing upon that sublimely gorgeous face, you were struck by the fact that she was even more beautiful in person. Yes, the camera and screen did not—and how silly it sounds to say—do Elizabeth Taylor justice.

Looking at each other, I could feel palpitation. (Mine, of course.)

Suddenly I was all thumbs, but figured she was probably used to having that effect, and that relaxed me. Some.

What was nice about her was that she seemed to be genuinely enjoying the moment, fascinated by the trick and earnestly and conscientiously following my instructions. A less classy celebrity might have clowned and tried to screw me up.

Then I said something I regretted.

On about the fourth cut-and-restore, she had some trouble severing the rope and I heard myself say, "You can cut it, Miss Taylor. Just think of it as the marital bond." She was so concentrated I hoped she might have missed it.

There was a noticeable murmur of disapproval from a few, but before I had completed a wince, thanks to whatever gods may be, she laughed.

Heartily is hardly the word. The Taylor laugh wasn't just any laugh; certainly not that of a refined lady. She gave out with the great full-throated guffaw known to her friends. It was a robust and delightfully bawdy thing, more appropriate to a stevedore than a beauty.

The renowned Liz Laugh was surely part of what endeared her to crews and stagehands, with whom she liked to exchange ribald humor the way Carole Lombard did, both of them reportedly preferring to hang out with "the workers"—the folk Joan Crawford graciously referred to when accepting an Oscar as "the little people behind the scenes"—rather than with their illustrious colleagues.

My late wife, the actress Carrie Nye, made a dreadful movie called *Divorce His, Divorce Hers* with the Burtons in 1973. She was a gifted writer, and when she got back from Germany—where the movie was made for some Burton-related tax reasons—she penned, for friends' amusement, a comic piece called "Making It in Munich." It's laugh-out-loud funny.

My friend Chris Porterfield read it and passed it to Henry Grunwald, then the top editor at *Time*, who said, "This goes in the next issue." *Time* introduced the piece by saying that Miss Nye had appeared with the glam pair in the two-part movie, adding that, "incredibly," it was about to be rebroadcast.

Carrie Nye was especially pleased when Gore Vidal called with praise, complaining, "I can't get things *Time* asks me to write into the magazine and you get in without trying."

She liked both Burtons, saying she felt sorry for Elizabeth and that, being from the South, she knew the problems of women married to alcoholics. We never knew if either of them read "Making It in Munich." The piece's humor derived from such matters as the director's awful dilemmas, like the fact that by the time Liz got to the studio, Richard would be too drunk to continue work, while her own hearty imbibing disqualified her by the time he sobered up. A dilemma because they had scenes together and simultaneous sobriety was rare. I think my favorite line was about the beleaguered director, "who was 4 ft. 11 in. tall, or at least he was when we began."

At the risk of a sudden change of tone, you can be sure that legions envied them their fabulous, in the true sense of the word, lives. (For astonishing details, see the page-turner book *Furious Love*.)

Think how many folks would say they'd trade their own dreary lives in an instant to have been one of Those Two. The glamour, the celebrity, the adoring (and often life-and-limb-threatening) throngs, the caviar and champagne, the travel, the passel of dogs and children hauled along, the sex, the yachts, the mansions and castles and whole floors of hotels, the walnut-sized diamonds and rubies . . .

But before making that somewhat Mephisophelean bargain, I would caution those who'd readily shed their own drab existence to be Liz or Dick to think twice. You're talking about a woman plagued all her life with ten people's medical horrors, heroically endured. He, too, had awful illnesses, some not publicly known. Like hemophilia and epilepsy.

We're also talking about two greatly gifted people, of course. Also about two drunks, constant smokers, spouse dumpers, and pill takers, reckless with their health and often with their careers; with Richard—who at one point would put away three bottles of vodka a day—dead in his fifties.

I feel lucky to have crossed paths with them. She was wonderful and he was wonderful.

To envy them you have to be nuts.

MARCH 25, 2011

In Defense of Offense

B rief dialogue:

Network executive: We're afraid some viewers might be
  offended.
D.C.: So?

Thus began, with my shocking impertinence, my first lesson in
network nervousness.

It couldn't have come at a more discouraging time. I had just
finished taping my very first show on ABC.

I was proud of the lineup of guests I had managed to snare
for the scary maiden voyage on the stormy seas of hosting a
ninety-minute talk show. The guests booked were three distinct
personalities. What is known in the talk show game as "a good mix."
Muhammad Ali, Angela Lansbury, and Gore Vidal.

The talk was brisk and lively and there was much gratifying
laughter from the studio audience. I came offstage relieved not to
be dripping flop sweat and delighted to have the first one down and
at having it go so well.

I expected a cheery slap on the back from the network man, and
more or less got it. Only it was applied elsewhere.

"Nobody gives a goddamn what Muhammad Ali and Gore
Vidal think about the Vietnam war."

Shock preceded anger.

Hadn't I done what I was supposed to do? Booked remarkable

guests, kept the conversational ball in the air, and entertained the viewers?

Apparently not.

I asked what it was about the show I had just done that the network could be worried about.

"We just don't want to offend anyone," he said to my wondering ears. So that was it. Someone somewhere might be offended.

I've never quite understood why this word—"offended"—is so horrifying. What doesn't offend *somebody*? And who wants to see, read, or write anything that is simon-pure in its inability to offend those dreaded "someones"?

"What could be more offensive than an offense-free show?" I sincerely inquired of the network suit.

That was considered offensive.

My favorite first dose of offended reaction is one I may have reported here before. It came from an apparently ruffled resident of Waco, Texas. My secretary was reluctant to show it to me. Handprinted in pencil and all in caps, it read: DEAR DICK CAVETT YOU LITTLE SAWED OFF FAGGOT COMMUNIST SHRIMP.

A lot of thought went into that.

Untypically, there was a return address and I shot right back, "I am not sawed-off."

Anyone working in the media can tell you that there seems to be an always-ready-to-explode segment of the populace for whom offense is a fate worse than anything imaginable. You'd think offense is one of the most calamitous things that could happen to a human being; right up there with the loss of a limb, or just missing a parking space.

What is our obligation to the offendees? To help them limit their suffering by avoiding all offense? With what advice?

You could stay in the house, watch no TV, read nothing of any kind including potentially upsetting snail mail or e-mail, and you just might manage to glide through an offense-free day. No surly neighbor, no near misses by unpunished, demented, sidewalk-riding cyclists, no cabdriver letting other cabs in ahead of yours while distractedly nattering on his phone in no known language. Stay cocooned and you will risk no insults from rude waiters, no pain from gruff clerks, no snarls from any employees of United Airlines.

"What sort of thing offends you, Mr. Cavett?" an interviewer asked me recently. "In other words, what to you is politically incorrect?"

"Anything that is politically correct."

Such as?

Well, the infantilism of the phrase "the *n* word," for example, and of those of less than fully formed cerebral development who have bowdlerized Mark Twain's masterpiece because of the references to Huck's beloved friend Jim as a "nigger," in the authentic vernacular of the time. I hate to spoil the fun of the benighted and alleged educators who have even pulled this great book from the school shelves, but Jim is the moral center of the story.

Presumably those same people would deny students the pleasure of Joseph Conrad's *The* [what? "Person of Color"?] *of the "Narcissus."* Why endow a word everyone knows with such majestic power that, like Yahweh of the Old Testament, it cannot be uttered?

A current example of offense ready to spring is the reaction of some to Julian Schnabel's remarkable and stirring new movie, *Miral*. Anything set in the always simmering Middle East is going to be a lightning rod. But the nay-saying here is upsetting.

Taken from Rula Jebreal's excellent novel of the same name, much of the expressed heavy criticism of it is all wrong. The movie has had rained upon it the ire of the offense brigade. (Embarrassingly, some prominent Jewish organizations have not felt the need to see it in order to denounce it. Others, though, have praised it.)

Those who take *Miral* as an out-and-out political screed don't seem to get it. It's a dramatic rendering of the life of a girl caught up in a troubled world of violent passions. Not, as some fevered detractors have seen it, a venomous assault on Israel.

I have at least two sets of friends who've announced that they are definitely not going to see the movie.

I was taken aback. "Shouldn't you have seen the movie in order to be able to say that?" I said, jesting partially, inspired perhaps by Mark Twain's opinion that three specific literary scholars who lavishly praised James Fenimore Cooper's writing might have done well to read some of it.

As to *Miral*, I suggest you see it.

How sad when art is viewed through a dreary political lens. In a world with a better grip on itself, the proper reaction to Schnabel's and Jebreal's touching movie would be, "What a hell of a good story!"

I hope that doesn't hurt anyone's feelings.

APRIL 15, 2011

The Week That Was

This is not the column I was going to write, but because of the recent days of relentless saturation—and I don't mean by or about the Mississippi River—whatever I try to type, my fingers, unbidden, produce the letters "Osama bin" etc.

Will the day ever come when we will find it hard to recall his name?

My first unwholesome thought was, "I hope he knew he was being killed." And not, say, shot in the head from behind while thinking pleasant thoughts, or enjoying a Nestlé's, and so going bye-bye without ever realizing that his goose was well done.

Did he cry out? Try for a gun? Utter anything?

And if he heard gunfire downstairs, why didn't he have a gun to hand? We know from that old piece of stock footage we're all heartily sick of that he can fire one.

Reaction has been all over the psychological map: somber, gleeful, humorous, nitpicky, and with plenty of food for lunatic obsessions.

On *The Daily Show*, Jon Stewart wittily showcased what will easily win the trophy in the "All-Time Dumbest Remarks by a Politician" category. We're treated to seeing former Pakistani president Pervez Musharraf defensively insist that had his country been complicit in hiding bin Laden, they would not have been dumb enough to put him in so prominent and discoverable a place. It required but a portion of the Stewart astuteness to illuminate the point: "So the

ISI [Inter-Services Intelligence] is way too smart to put bin Laden in such an obvious place, but far too clueless to know he was there."

Stewart followed this by showing a clip of the same hapless gent guesting on the show several years ago. Jon greets Musharraf with great civility, politely offers him a cup of tea from his native land, and begins, genially, "Where's Osama bin Laden?" There should be some sort of award for that.

I wouldn't be surprised if there's a word in German for having but two choices, both disastrous. Our weak "dilemma" isn't up to the job. I'm thinking, of course, of Pakistan's uncomfortable choice of being either a fool or a knave. Either (a) they sheltered bin Laden or (b) they were too incompetent to detect him. (Could someone closer to school days than I identify this as, perhaps, Logic 101's "law of excluded middle"?)

I'm surprised no one has suggested a second raid on Pakistan, this time with an Airbus to extract some of the billions of dollars we have sunk into this sinkhole. (I don't mean to offend.)

Eight feet to my right on TV it's being announced that an angry Pakistan is threatening to cut off future intelligence sharing with the United States. Who at Comedy Central is writing their stuff? More intelligence from the crack apparatus that gave us the hit song "I Wonder Who Lives in That Mansion."

I keep looking back at one photo. What, as distinct from what we are told, was that group of fascinated viewers in the White House Situation Room, watching the thing go down with such rapt expressions, actually watching? Was Hillary Clinton, covering her mouth, witnessing (as they say in the porno film business) "the money shot"?

Will commentators ever tire of irritating clichés like "laid their lives on the line" and "willing to die for the cause" and "ready to sacrifice their lives for our security"? Wouldn't it be refreshing to hear one of the heroic SEALs say, "Thanks for the praise, but like hell I was willing to die. I was there to stay alive and get the goddamn job done. Dead, I'm of limited use to my buddies. And my family."

And has political correctness struck here already? Headlines along the lines of NATIVE AMERICANS ANGERED BY "GERONIMO" have appeared. As a sort of honorary American Indian (adopted in both Sioux and Crow ceremonies), I'm surprised I wasn't offended. But it never occurred to naïve me that giving bin Laden the code name "Geronimo" in this cleanly executed raid wasn't in fact homage to the brave Chiricahua Apache so adept at raiding and killing his enemies—those Mexican and U.S. troops who had killed his wife, children, and people.

(To a man, my Indian friends deplore that PC, euphemistic, illogical, stillborn label "Native American." My friend John Running Hawk: "All my life we've been 'Indian people.' Now they're telling Indian people we aren't even Indians.")

One reporting highlight: Brian Williams rephrasing his question a third time before getting Leon Panetta to admit that waterboarding was involved. (Pass this technique on to some colleagues, Brian.)

At times like this I wish I were back in my old Socratic-style humanist philosopher Paul Weiss's class at Yale, seeing his lightning mind and mouth fire questions and field them from his charges. The air would be thick with provokers like *Is there such a thing as a purely evil act? What does it mean to forgive? Is the sacrifice of something of infinite value—a human life—ever justified for a* possible *good outcome? Can you call anything justice without due process? Do we want young people taught that execution without trial can be called justice? And by a president who is a constitutional scholar? When is it okay to shoot an unarmed man? Would offering him a gun make it moral? Is torture ever justified? Particularly when it yields so much destructively false information?*

You hate to take any of the fun out of this by impertinently wondering whether, since the chance of error and catastrophic failure was so high (cf. poor Jimmy Carter), a president with an approval rating of, say, 86 percent might have been less likely to risk it. And maybe the most intriguing question of all: Could this mission, if it had failed utterly, have been kept secret?

Please consider these, and have your paper on my desk by Friday.

MAY 6, 2011

The First Shall Be Last—or, Anyway, Second

Whoops. I've misinformed you.
I didn't mean to.

It happened in the recent column about political correctness. I love the fact that that particular column and subject drew from your side so many gratifying, sometimes vehement, well-written, and impressively thoughtful responses.

What you might call my unintended deception had to do with the incident in which the network man denounced (why don't I just go ahead and say "hated" and see if the heavens stay up?) my very first network *Dick Cavett Show*.

It turns out it was at once different from and worse than that.

An unearthed folder of stuff from that time reminds me of the true story. And incidents like this cause you to ponder the alleged fact, in current studies of that most fascinating of phenomena, memory, that we forget 80 percent of our past life. (Resisting joke about what other part of your life could you forget but the past part?)

And will they ever discover what determines what gets remembered and what doesn't? Why can I recall the words, and melody, to an ancient shampoo commercial ("Dream girl, dream girl, beautiful Lustre Creme girl"), my cousin's 1948 Michigan license plate number (JV 81 56), the full names of all my teachers from kindergarten through college (one friend remembers none), but not where I ate last night? What says, "Okay, this item goes in the Permanent Recall box and this into the Burn box?"

Now, where was I?

Ah, yes. So here, in the vernacular of the period, is what really went down at ABC in memory-dimmed 1968.

My original report is accurate as far as it goes. Coming off the set after somehow surviving the nerve-shredding ordeal of taping my very first live-on-tape, no-stopping, *ninety-minute* talk show (it took real men to do talk shows in those days), a show that had gone beautifully and was full of laughs, a man from the Nervous Executive Harassment Department summed up the accomplishment with "Nobody gives a goddamn what Muhammad Ali and Gore Vidal think about the Vietnam war."

Recovering from shock enough to point out that the audience did, and that Angela Lansbury, the other guest, had, and that the scary subject had occupied but a brief fragment of the whole show, didn't help. It only further tightened his grim visage.

Now for the part repressed—and maybe also suppressed—by Mnemosyne, lovely goddess of memory.

"This is not the show we bought," issued from the bloodless lips. "We can't air this as your first show." (Debut day was still a week hence.)

"What do you plan to do, then?" my agent, the legendary Sam Cohn, inquired in a controlled tone.

"We'll have to tape another show and put it on first and this one second. We can't risk this one for the first time out of the box."

Whether from bravery or career-ending tendency, I inquired in as polite a tone as I could muster, "And at that point will you stop being chickenshit?"

Well, boys and girls, under protest we did tape another show. And on the following Monday it aired as the first show. Happily, most reviewer types had decided to wait for more than just one show to write about the new program. They knew nothing, of course, about the first show / second show scheduling switcheroo.

You guessed it.

One reviewer said that the "first" show was a bit of a disappointment, that I seemed a touch dispirited, but that the "second" show was a pip, that I'd hit my stride in only a day. Of course, thanks to the network's timidity, those who *did* review the first show they saw got the duller one as my "opening night."

Funny, but pathetic, isn't it?

What can we learn from this?

Similar incidents lay ahead. Vietnam, of course, remained a continuing sore subject, producing cold sweats on the brows of my overseers. But it was impossible to avoid a subject that screamed at you daily. Unless, of course, you went out of your way and did a show about nothing more controversial than puppies, kitties, recipes, and how to embroider a dirndl. (I thought about it.)

But I learned to prevent secreting excess stomach acid by having the occasional war supporter on, for "balance," after guests had denounced that war we lost. (The wretched one that LBJ had formerly and famously referred to in the later regretted line that it was "a war for Asian boys.")

Having Buckley or Goldwater, or much less desirable types than these two real charmers, would, I was told, help pacify complainers (and life-and-limb threateners) and calm the FCC, not to mention keep stations from losing their licenses; all of it having to do with what the network told me was the "equal time requirement." This was bull. "Equal time," someone eventually pointed out to me, had to do only with political campaigns. So much for "Your guest bad-mouthed fly-fishing and I demand equal time." (Do you think I'm kidding?) And individual stations could "retain their licenses" by airing other shows, or shows of their own, on controversial subjects.

Before I knew that, I made waves for myself by saying what a silly idea "equal time" was anyway. An effective speaker can do more damage or more good in a well-stated minute than an angry klutz—poorly chosen to respond—could do in half an hour.

Although recalling these things right now has increased my pulse and given me the vapors, I must admit I loved it when the ice got thin. I gradually eased into the realization that the occasional challenging of a guest could produce "good television" and the viewers loved it. As when I said to the LSD-advocating T. Leary, "You know, I really think you're full of crap." The powers left that in, to my surprise, probably because it would play well with right-wing complainers. (Would they have been so reasonable had I said it to, oh, Spiro Agnew?)

How silly to have thought when the first show / second show problem slipped into the past that from now on it would be only smooth sailing.

Ahead lay: Lester Maddox's walk-off when I declined to apologize; the Chicago Seven, and the press's saving that show upon learning the network was going to bury it; Gore and Norman; Lily Tomlin's abrupt departure from the stage, protesting a male star of minimal forehead area whose sexist remarks appalled her; veterans for and against the war (John Kerry, e.g.); at least one murderer (Jeffrey MacDonald, of *Fatal Vision* fame); Jane Fonda and Mark Lane on purported atrocities by U.S. soldiers; Lillian Hellman suing Mary McCarthy and, oh yes, me; John and Yoko singing "Woman Is the Nigger of the World" and the flap it caused (for another time); and on and on.

And just while wondering what else could possibly happen that hadn't, the on-camera death of J. I. Rodale, which, as the Brits say, "just about put the tin lid on it."

But I loved it when the ice got thin.

As Dr. Samuel Johnson said about facing the gallows, "It focuses the mind wonderfully."

MAY 20, 2011

Waiting (and Waiting) in the Wings

Y ou forget it can happen.

You finally get tickets to the show you've been dying to see, you settle into your seat—and it happens. The dread announcement.

An amplified voice from backstage utters those awful words: "For this performance, the part of _____ will be played by _____."

Before the sentence ends, a groan goes up from the entire audience. The moment is bad for them, but infinitely worse for one person standing backstage who hears it clearly. The one who, somewhere earlier in the day, has been told, "You're going on tonight." The one who has not yet made an entrance but has already, in effect, been booed. Hearing the dismal reaction at the mention of his name is enough to shrivel the soul.

Meanwhile, out front in your hard-to-come-by seat, self-pity hits hard. You've read what a great team the two lead actors make, and it's as if, in a far-off time, you were told that Mr. Hardy had been taken ill and you'd be seeing Laurel & Jenkins. Why, you wonder, did this have to happen to me? I finally get tickets to *The Book of Mormon* and I have to endure an understudy. (Technically, in this case, a "standby.")

The actor missing is invariably one you've looked forward to, and who's been praised to the skies. The wonderful comic actor Josh Gad had awakened with the actor's nightmare: an absent voice.

(The other male lead, by the way, is the impeccable Andrew Rannells.)

Sorrow and self-pity were short-lived. Another splendid actor, Jared Gertner, entered for Gad and instantly won the hearts of the disappointed. And held those hearts right through to the big, rewarding moment at the end—the one that surely makes up for standing backstage and hearing the announcement of your name trigger a groan—the curtain call. There's a big surge in the cheering as you take your solo bow and your onstage fellow players salute you for having not just somehow gotten through it, but gotten through it with distinction.

He looks delightfully funny. Bulky of upper body (padded, possibly) and with legs appearing barely adequate to support their load, topped by oddly orange hair that fits the head like an ample, folded-under hat of some sort, Gertner exudes comic presence.

His physical movements reach back to the eccentric and hilarious ones of the skilled vaudeville comedians of another time. Where did he acquire them? In any case, Jared Gertner won't be a standby forever.

There are actors who love such a job. A friend of mine stood by for a star for a year and went on only twice.

"Best job I ever had," he said then. "I have a place to go at night, I get a nice check, I'm in the world I love, I schmooze with my fellow actors, catch up with all the latest gossip, and I sit in a dressing room with a good book. This month I've read four great novels I cheated myself out of in school with CliffsNotes."

In Henry Fonda's more than a thousand performances on Broadway in *Mister Roberts*, reports Fonda's daughter Jane, he had a series of standbys. Not one ever set foot on the stage.

Someone said the best way to vanish from show business was to be Ethel Merman's understudy.

Merman famously never missed a performance, saying, "I'm gonna take a chance on some young cutie going out there and being better than me? Fat chance!" (The printable version of the quote.)

A lady I know who stood by for the indestructible dynamo in *Call Me Madam* was warned, "If a cement truck hits Ethel she goes on." (Some would pity the truck.)

Mormon is not a show for dummies. Like *South Park*, from the same intrepid pair—Trey Parker and Matt Stone—it is chock full of allusions, paraphrases, and, yes, classical references enough to delight the well-read and educated. And, as in *South Park*, they come thick and fast, especially in the sparkling lyrics.

The production sails through the evening at such a hilarious clip that you dread the inevitable duller spots that any show has. They never come. And I've never laughed harder.

Is it actorproof, as one critic erred in asserting? Nothing is. I've been distressed this year by an alarming trend in my beloved Broadway theater that wasn't so before: seeing largely fine shows, with otherwise good casts, in each of which are from one to three actors who appear to have mugged someone for their Equity cards. There's no excuse for this in a city where *Law & Order* for years proved how many countless splendid actors we have. (Will someone please explain this?) If *Mormon* appears actorproof, it's because there isn't one clunker in the company. This may be a recent record.

On the way to seeing the show, I had one trepidation. Was it conceivable that I could be offended?

As one who has railed in these columns against political correctness and who maintains that being offended is a witless waste of time, I wondered, could this show test my limits? But denunciation of the show, as far as I can tell, must have been confined solely to those who have not seen it, a practice much in fashion these days. (Maybe the show's having been laden with Tony Awards earlier this week will encourage some naysayers to at least have a peek. Maybe with an aisle seat, in case their fears are confirmed.)

The evening is a virtual encyclopedia of that strictly American contribution to the world, the Broadway musical. Homages, references, parodies, and allusions in all the art forms of the musical—choreography, sets, costumes, lighting, music, and lyrics—are there throughout. (The guy in the next seat enjoyed ticking them off: "Robbins, Fosse, Busby, Rodgers and Hammerstein.") Movie allusions also abound.

So, finally, how do you present sacrilege, irreverence, blasphemy, and lots of dirty words onstage and get away with it? Apparently it is done by some mysterious alchemy whereby truths and profundities somehow come through all the frivolity and escapism.

This remarkable work inspires the thought that every religion springs from two universal needs: to explain the origin of the human race and to be comforted about the harsh finality and loss that is death. Whether this involves pyramids, seventy-two virgins, healing frogs, burning bushes, walking on water, or tribes of alien forebears, the camaraderie, the mythologies, and the comfort factors are about the same. Different religions—each of which always claims to have a monopoly on the truth—work for different people. (Is that too profound?)

The good news is that *Book of M.* will be around a long time. The only physical danger in seeing the show is that you might laugh your head off.

Finally, there is a strange irony afoot.

The evening has touching, tender moments. And for all its themes and targets—traditional faiths, religious hypocrisy, icky sanctimony, corrupt religiosity, bizarre sexuality—the show has by some ingenious trickery co-opted one of the supposed virtues of going to church. Considering the fineness of everything you see and hear combined with the buoyancy of a cast of actors who seem to be having the time of their lives, you leave feeling exhilarated, renewed, uplifted, and full of something alarmingly akin to—brace yourself—faith.

That is its magic.

JUNE 17, 2011

I Owe William Jennings Bryan an Apology

Three fifteen p.m.

Certainly among the most delicious of childhood and early schooldays memories is that magical moment when the standard old-fashioned classroom clock with the Roman numerals at long last clicked to that magic rightward position: 3:15.

That moment was great on any day, but couldn't hold a candle to the one accompanied by the words "Have a nice summer."

Three solid months of NO SCHOOL!!

Three months of leisurely reading what you *wanted* to read. In my case, *Penrod* for the fifth or sixth time; all the Sherlock Holmes stories, again; both Tom and Huck; all books on Japan and Indians and magic. And Nancy Drew. I doubt that any of my male friends or I would admit to one another that last-named item, but there it is.

Summer meant mischief. Blowing up people's mailboxes around the Fourth with two-inchers from China. ("Instructions: Lay on ground. Light fuse. Retire quickly.")

And it seemed that most summers would contain something truly outlandish—and sometimes dangerous and destructive—dreamed up by me, or Tom Keene, or Marvin Breslow, or Hugh McKnight, or the now dead and longed-for-in-memory Jimmy Mc-Connell, my personal Huck Finn.

One such incident—wince-making in recall—contained all the desired elements: some devious plotting, borderline—and sometimes south of the border—illegality, "minor" destruction of property, and excitement enhanced by virtue of its being committed under cover of darkness.

And not least the tantalizing possibility of once again experiencing the fun of eluding ("ditching") an unwelcome squad car.

A bit of history: While my companions in malfeasance and I were all in high school, somebody decided to adorn the majestic front steps of Lincoln's Nebraska state capitol building with a statue. Not a statue of some ancient mythical figure, or a sculptor's rendering of some unnamed "God of Wisdom" or "The Spirit of Law," but—for mysterious reasons—William Jennings Bryan. A bronze, virtually black (remember that) eight- or ten-foot statue of the great "Prophet from Nebraska," as he was derided by Clarence Darrow in the Scopes trial.

W.J.B. was caught by the sculptor in full oratorical pose, arm in the air, proclaiming. Perhaps the famous gem of his cultured windiness, the "Cross of Gold" speech?

We will answer their demand for a gold standard by saying to them: "You shall not press down upon the brow of labor this crown of thorns, you shall not crucify mankind upon a cross of gold."

Plopping Bryan on the capitol steps bred anger in the community. Fiery letters swarmed. "It looks like our great capitol building is dedicated to this mediocrity," read a typical protest missive to the editor of the *Lincoln Journal*.

We hatched a plot of action. I think it was born in the brains of two friends of mine, Roger Henkle and / or Marvin Breslow. At this distance—considering the "whew!" factor of what might have happened to us all—I don't know whether to assign their scheme praise or blame.

Neither fellow was the sort mothers feared their child might associate with. A year older than I, they seemed better educated then than I feel now, and both went on to distinguished academic careers in "fancy eastern schools" (like Harvard).

Sadly, they had to—I confess it—fill me in on who Bryan was: booming-voiced orator, U.S. congressman from Nebraska, thrice-failed candidate for president, ardent Prohibitionist, and vehement enemy of Darwinism for religious reasons in the famous Scopes trial.

My knowledge was limited to knowing there was a hospital named for him in Lincoln.

I have no idea which or what combination of these facts about "the Great Commoner" made us decide his looming presence on the capitol steps required attack.

But our goofy enthusiasm for an assault on poor old Bryan grew. Fortunately, we had no access to dynamite or nitroglycerine. We settled on a less violent course.

Whitewash.

We agreed on a night. There were but three malefactors in the car. Henkle and Breslow had to miss our D-Day for some kind of graduation ceremony, I think it was. But we had set our date and seemed possessed with some sort of near-fanaticism so gripping that, probably, like Macbeth's hired murderers (paraphrasing), our spirits shined through us.

Dickie A. (nod to possible statute of limitations) drove. We pulled up about half a block away from the front of the capitol's four-hundred-foot tower, irreverently nicknamed by numerous would-be wits "the Penis of the Plains," with a direct view of the offending Colossus of Bryan.

Monroe U. supplied the disfiguring liquid. (If the case still had life in it, I'm sure even Inspector Clouseau would be able to discover the probable number of Monroe U.'s in my class.)

On the night of nights, three of us pulled up about a half block from the front of the building. I can still summon the tingling thrill of sitting there in the car, about to commit our nasty bit of mischief ("crime" seems a bit strong, but then—).

For a moment, we all sat in a sort of meditative silence. There was only the rustling of the breeze in the elm trees—that wonderful background sound effect that, in memory, still evokes the adventures of summer nights and misdeeds in the delicious dark.

"Well, let's get this show on the road!" said Monroe U., and I thought he sounded like John Wayne in *Sands of Iwo Jima*.

The stars and partial moon lent just enough light to make out the figure of Monroe, slinking away in the dark. We could just see him making his way toward the illustrious victim, toting what must have been at least a two-gallon can of a home-brewed, gooey combination of whitewash and real white paint.

In the dim light, Monroe faded more. Then we could just barely see him crouch below the base of the statue, then straighten.

Suddenly—seemingly in slow motion—what looked like a beautiful, gleaming, lengthening white ghost rose eerily before the dark figure of Bryan. It glided gracefully upward into the air. And then froze in place.

In the car, someone taking French said, "Fait accompli."

We quickly gathered Monroe and his empty vessel into the car, and I think it's then we started to get scared. An uneasy night's sleep followed.

Arising early, I drove in alone to see our handiwork. Maybe it would be barely noticeable. Or have evaporated to nothing. No such luck.

The eloquent and pompous orator had been robbed of all dignity. It looked as if, perhaps in mid-declamation, he had vomited on himself.

Voluminously. Stark white-on-black.

One vast splotch was at about chest level, with nasty drippings down the coat and trouser legs. Dignity was cruelly besmirched.

I went and got Marvin, telling him only that I had a surprise for him. I didn't tell him we had actually done it. We approached the rudely decorated orator and he blurted, "You really did it!"

As we passed right in front of the spectacle—and I didn't want to be spotted lingering there too long—what looked like almost life-threatening paroxysms of laughter seized Marvin. We were both in hysterics as he took off his glasses to dab tears.

We hadn't anticipated the next surprise. We stopped at the

Cornhusker Hotel for coffee and there it was on the newsstand. The early-bird edition of the *Lincoln Journal*, front page, upper-right corner. A good-sized picture of our handiwork with the caption "Bryan Sloshed."

I've lost my beloved copy. If the now-named *Lincoln Journal Star* can find it, I'll pass it on, perhaps in my next confession from my criminal past.

Under the caption, it went on to say (more or less, if memory serves), "Early risers on their way to church services were greeted by a startling sight. Vandals had been at work. The controversial statue of William Jennings Bryan had been sloshed with white paint." Etc.

It was starting to get scary. Thoughts of our parents intruded on the fun, and mine were teachers in the Lincoln school system.

But, happily, the tale pretty much dwindles away here. We were not caught. (Unless we are now.) There was one chilling moment at school when someone not connected to the thing whispered, passing in the hall, "Nice going," causing me to recall the Wordsworth line, "Shades of the prison-house begin to close / Upon the growing Boy." Lincoln High Schoolers from back then still ask me if I had anything to do with it.

Lest you worry about me and my flawed character, I'm not what you would call proud of this dumb prank.

But I wouldn't have missed it for the world.

Poor old Willy Bryan's frock coat and trousers and shoes and pedestal were cleansed, and after a while he was no longer there at all.

What a distant world it is from today's, in which kids don't slosh statues, they hack computers. We're probably lucky that in those primitive times, before even the electric typewriter, there was no possible e-mail trail for our prosecutable stunt.

Am I foolish to feel glad I was a kid then, rather than now? The "now" when a sixteen-year-old recently said to me, "I doubt that any of my friends and I have ever seen a black-and-white movie."

There's a singular aftermath.

Years later, on one of my weekend theater-district-haunting trips down from Yale (all the real men spent their weekends at Smith or Vassar), there, coming out of a restaurant, was the wonderful actor Ed Begley (Sr.).

I'd just seen him as the loudmouth bigot in the film *Twelve Angry Men*. Suddenly, I had a strange, momentary urge that I couldn't explain: the urge to apologize to him for something. And then the sensation clarified, explaining why I didn't, in my usual manner, walk up and meet him.

I had seen him a year earlier on Broadway with Paul Muni in *Inherit the Wind*.

He had played the William Jennings Bryan role.

JULY 8, 2011

Sorry, W.J.B., to Bring This Up Again

You—collectively, and perhaps you specifically—delighted me with your thoughtful and articulate responses to my confessional column involving the William Jennings Bryan jape committed by me and my rascally friends.

It always fascinates me when your replies range widely among delighted glee, reported laughs out loud, puzzlement, prim disapproval, outright excoriation, and those from readers willing to throw themselves between me and the snarls of the e-mailer "spikethedog."

At least I can fulfill a promise. You may have already noted, below, the photo I hoped last time I might be able to unearth to verify the lamentable deed. (A few suggested I had made the whole thing up, which, if true, would now include an ingenious bit of Photoshopping.)

Anyway, it appears on the following page, thanks to the well-run archives of the *Lincoln* (Neb.) *Journal Star*.

Marv Breslow, whom you met in the original column, and I are both recovering from the shared realization that we are the only remaining survivors of the dubious project.

Our reactions were various. We were both pleased that our lamented buddy-in-crime, the late Roger Henkle, who went on to better use of his fine mind at Harvard, was touchingly recognized by name by surprised and admiring former students of his at Brown.

Others deserving a place on this somewhat-less-than-honorable-mention list were Dickie Andrews, who went into, ironically, the

Lincoln Journal Star

law, and the only one of us who could supply the necessary parents' car; Charles Beans (Lincoln High School–mate, then Princeton), who had to attend a prom but financed the paint expenditure; and Monroe Usher, the only one of us with the apparent strength, coordination, and physical adroitness to accomplish the "delivery" of the viscous white substance, which the photo shows was voluminous and must have weighed half a ton.

Both Marv and I were shocked at the photo. Neither of us remembered anywhere near accurately how much paint was really dispatched Bryanward, thinking it had been more like one big blotch on the Great Commoner's coat.

Not something that looked as though he had collided with a tank truck of the gleaming substance.

What I didn't misreport last time was that, driving by and viewing our handiwork clearly for the first time in broad daylight the following sunny morning, I had to pull over and park the car because further driving would have been hazardous to our health, so helplessly dissolved in boyish laughter were we.

A few readers, deploring the escapade, wondered if it ever occurred to my allegedly bright mind back then what some of the consequences might have been if we'd been caught. Shamefully, it hadn't until just about now.

My wife, Martha, although entertained by the story, chilled me with "There would have been no Yale."

Yikes!

Everything in my life after high school until today stems from the Yale scholarship, the unexpected thing that got me to the world of my dreams and yearnings: the east, New York, theater, showbiz, television, everything I was sure, then, I wanted. (And just think. You would be reading someone else right now. A disturbing thought. But at least it wouldn't be *News of the World*.)

But would arrest have spelled calamity for all of us? Meaning, would the University of Nebraska and Yale and in fact all of our respective schools have taken the fatal view of this blot on our record? A few readers assure me that that would certainly happen with today's schools and in these times—with schoolkids pleading for the erasure from their record of even a minor infraction that would doom any chance at college for them.

Was it always thus? Or were we lucky to have lived in a more relaxed, lenient, less disapproving time, when college admission was not cutthroat? Marvin was smart enough, he now admits, to have worried about this at the time. I, not so much.

Who knows? Suppose we had been pinched by John Law. Instead of passing on into the glory days of college, we might both have found ourselves flipping hamburgers at KenEddy's Drive-in, out on O Street in Lincoln. And then gone on to lesser things.

Before kissing this subject good-bye (as some of you have done to me for telling this story), I have one other chore.

Should there, to my surprise, prove to be a hereafter, I might be wise to work up and have handy a couple of things to say, just in case I run into, in the Sweet By and By, the imposing (statuesque?) figure of W.J.B. himself standing before me. I'll need something to say when he casts a steely gaze upon me and intones, "*Well*, young Mr. Cavett!"

(I will not bring up the subject of his cleaning bills.)

JULY 29, 2011

Flying? Increasingly for the Birds

"I'll be passing the back of my hand over your buttocks and then come up the insides of your legs up toward the private parts. Is that okay?"

"Sounds peachy to me," I knew not to say. You're not supposed to joke with airport security, as people have learned the hard way.

This makes sense, but as with so much about airport security—or as someone has called it, "Security Theater"—it seems a bit silly. Are terrorists known for their tendency to joke? (Is there a paperback called *Jokes for Jihadists?*)

When you refuse, as I do, to be ordered into the big scanner with its "safe" amount of X-ray, you are made to feel like a wimp and told to "Stand over there!" And over there—with maybe one or two others who have also noted that whatever X-rays you are urged to get in life are invariably "safe"—you stand, a little ashamed, waiting until the patter gets back from the toilet.

On a recent patting (and the patters, I should say, are a nice lot, picked perhaps for their demeanor), the description "toward the private parts" had a grain of inaccuracy. The rising hands didn't stop short, causing a slight "ow" on my part. "Sorry" was delivered feelingly (no pun intended).

Another time, after having been felt up in public, I fell into a pleasant chat with the man with the businesslike hands. He'd recognized me, and there were no other pattees waiting.

I asked, "What sort of jokes are you tiredest of by the one patted?"

"Oh, you can probably guess," my guy said cheerfully.

"Something like 'Hey, cute stuff, whatcha doin' after the show?'" I guessed.

"You got it."

"Any of the would-be humorists ask what sort of man would seek a job patting other men?"

"You got it again."

"How are you supposed to behave in the face of such wit?"

"Smile and keep patting."

I'm sure no professional patter lives in fear that an accumulation of such microerotic experiences will endanger his orientation. Or the passenger's.

As you know, if you endure the increasingly dismal experience of flying, some airports are markedly better than others.

Detroit Metro Airport deserves a valentine.

My wife, a million-miler out of Detroit from years lived in Ohio, views it as an oasis. The employees seem to have been picked for their helpfulness. And you never stand in a line that seems to stretch to the horizon while additional lanes are closed for no apparent reason. (Saving money with fewer employees?)

And the security is just plain better. They find things other places don't. A friend states, "I'm horrified at stuff I mistakenly put in my carry-on. And it's been missed everywhere. Except Detroit."

In my case, a lethal-looking metal letter opener stuck to the lining of my carry-on bag had passed undiscovered at various less diligent airports by who knows how many previous "inspectors." In Detroit it was rightly seized; but seized in a nice, unnecessarily apologetic—but professional—manner, rather than with that cold air of enjoyed power so often seen in the airport worker. Bringing to mind Shakespeare's "Dress'd in a little, brief authority."

A chilling note: Another affable patter in another major city, when I asked him if anyone was still dumb enough to try to get bad stuff through security, said, "Mr. Cavett, you'd be amazed at how many guns we get this way." I gulped and asked what would be happening to me now if I had one. "See that guy at the coffee counter? He's a cop. I raise my hand and next thing you know you're wearing his bracelets. You go away for a good long time." "Thanks," I said, too stunned to ask who those reckless heat toters were. From his manner it was clear they weren't merely licensed gun carriers who wear them all the time and just forgot.

Another thing about Detroit: they don't run out of those plastic tubs so you stand around in your stockings until a new load eventually arrives, apparently from another state.

Why should there be such a contrast between flying from Detroit and, say, from that bad dream posing as an airport, grubby LaGuardia?

Is there a director of some special genius behind the Detroit operation? If so, would that person please publish his secrets in a book and pass it around?

At LaGuardia, my wife, the seasoned traveler, dutifully presented the see-through plastic bag containing a few small bottles of the approved size containing liquid. One was seized. It contained something she valued. Pointing out that it was regulation size, she got, "It ain't labeled, lady."

Supposing whatever possibly dangerous substance it contained had, say, "olive oil" written on it, I inquired, then would it be okay?

"Yes."

"Do you see anything a little stupid about that?" I asked in my sunniest manner. He appeared not to. He dropped the bottle into the barrel beside him.

"One more question. Do you ever feel a little funny about standing eight inches from a barrel full of possible explosives for the rest of the day?"

He went into that mode of looking into the distance instead of at you. I leaned into his gaze, just for fun.

"Move on," he sort of belched.

Security Theater. That funhouse, LaGuardia.

AUGUST 19, 2011

The Great Melvino, or Our Mr. Brooks

Have you, perchance, decided—as I have—not to spend the weekend re-wallowing in 9/11 with the media? Aside from allowing Saint Rudolph, former tenant of Gracie Mansion, to trumpet once again his self-inflated heroism on that nightmare day, the worst feature of this relentlessly repeated carnival of bitter sights and memories is that *it glamorizes the terrorists.*

How they must enjoy tuning in to our festival of their spectacular accomplishments, cheering when the second plane hits and high-fiving when the falling towers are given full-color international showcasing for the tenth time.

Who wants this? Surveys show people want to forget it, or at least not have it thrust down their throats from all over the dial annually. It can't have to do with that nauseating buzzword "closure." There is no closure to great tragedies. Ask the woman on a call-in show who said how she resents all this ballyhooing every year of the worst day of her life: "My mother died there that day. I'm forced to go through her funeral again every year."

Is all this stuff a ratings bonanza? Who in the media could be that heartless?

Let's turn from tragedy to a somewhat lighter subject—say, comedy.

Years and years ago, when I was writing for Johnny Carson during the day, I was moonlighting (with permission) after sunset, beginning the fretful route to hoped-for comedy stardom in the prescribed starting place in those days: clubs and coffeehouses in Greenwich Village.

My manager, the great Jack Rollins, brought a woman from a big ad agency to catch my act at the Bitter End. I was beginning to develop some skill at ad-libbing, and my dealing with a heckler impressed her.

That's how, a few days later, I found myself in a recording studio across a table from—yikes!—Mel Brooks. I knew the name from his writer credit on *Your Show of Shows*, where, still mute and inglorious behind the scenes, Mel once had Carl Reiner ask Sid Caesar's German professor character what to do if your rope breaks while mountain climbing.

First he recommends, "Scream and keep screaming all the way down . . . this way they'll know where to find you."

Carl asks if there's maybe anything else you can do.

Caesar: Well, there's the other method. As soon as the rope breaks, you spread your arms and begin to fly.
Reiner: But humans can't fly.
Caesar: How do you know? You might be the first one. Anyway, you can always go back to screaming.

(This and much like it can be found in Ted Sennett's book *Your Show of Shows*.)

But I, and others, knew Mel big-time from the bestselling comedy album, *The 2,000-Year-Old Man*.

Ballantine Beer, starting a new commercial campaign, had hired Mel to be "the 2,500-Year-Old Brewmaster." They needed a Carl Reiner stand-in to interview the old gent, whose voice resembled, not entirely coincidentally, the 2,000-year-old man's.

I've never had more fun.

First, I stood around nervously. Then Mel Brooks himself walked into the studio. He eyed my slight, twentyish self with suspicion. "Spectacularly gentile!" he observed. We've been friends ever since.

There was not a word of script. The ad agency guy directing our sessions urged, "Just hit Mel with anything that comes to mind, the way Carl does. He's best when he doesn't know what's coming."

I played an eager young interviewer, bringing his hand mike to the old man's cave and peppering him with questions, challenges, skepticism, and, once, mock hurt feelings, asking,

D.C.: Why are you rude to me, sir?
M.B.: Why are you wearing a cardboard belt?

Example of a challenge:

D.C.: Sir, I don't think you've ever actually tasted the beer we're selling. Do so now.
M.B.: All right, Fluffy. (*Sipping sound: voop! voop!*)
D.C.: How would you put it, sir?
M.B.: My tongue just threw a party for my mouth!

I could never corner Mel. God knows I tried. I sat there and watched him go comic-mad before my wondering eyes, scoring every time he opened his mouth.

There was no dross. The first session went three hours, at the end of which both of us were exhausted but high.

Once an engineer in the control room laughed so hard he fell against the recording equipment and it had to be reset. Mel broke me up in such helpless laughter, and so many times, that the agency was forced—or someone was hip enough—to leave some of my laughter in. I've seen this faked, but it was obvious that I was genuinely convulsed by my partner.

If the raw, unedited tapes from which the commercials were cut are not preserved somewhere, it's comparable as a cultural loss to the burning of the library at Alexandria.

The commercials were loved. The agency said it had never gotten such a volume of fan mail as poured in from people mad for them, demanding to know when they were scheduled so as not to miss any. Men told their wives to listen all day and record them.

I decided I could soon retire, thanks to the storm of residual checks that jammed my mailbox.

But there was a problem.

The product was not equally adored. I was shown a letter from one fan: "I don't know how long I can afford picking up six-packs of Ballantine to keep those commercials on the air. It tastes like piss."

Soon, alas, the brewmaster and his young quizzer / tormentor were out of work. There are those who contrived to somehow collect the commercials. (They're on a DVD Mel and Carl put out for Shout! Factory.)

Happily, this greatly gifted man and I have been reunited. On HBO you can now catch a hilarious hour (yes, I do say so) called *Mel Brooks and Dick Cavett Together Again.*

It was an evening of seemingly nonstop laughter that we did together in a grand and glorious old theater in Los Angeles earlier this year. Mel had the wit to have it recorded.

A moment I'll never forget: standing backstage at the fifteen-hundred-seat showplace before we went on, I don't think either of us was full of confidence. Mel's in his eighties, and when I looked at him standing there with just a hint of a stoop, I thought, at this point in his life he may really need this to go well.

Suddenly, we were introduced from the stage. I looked at Mel. The stoop had vanished. "Hey, this might be fun," I said. Mel: "Good audience." I let Mel walk out first, and held for a bit as he was bathed in roaring applause. He dropped a couple of decades. Then I did much the same.

It was a case of two performers sparking each other. When Mel laughed at me—genuinely, not false breakup—I felt a surge and got better. It worked both ways and, of course, much of that mutual sparking had to do with mutual affection.

It might be illegal or something for me to quote from the

program—though I will say that the conversation and stories ranged from Alfred Hitchcock to Cary Grant to Mel's theatrical debut—so let me have a free go at your funny bone with an earlier recollection from Mel.

Years back, I tuned in once just in time to see Mel describing—almost certainly to Johnny Carson—how dismal were his nine months stuck in Yugoslavia shooting *The Twelve Chairs*. He said you couldn't really do anything at night "because all of Belgrade is lit by a ten-watt bulb. And you couldn't go anywhere because Tito had the car."

I remember laughing so hard I spilled something.

He went on to say that the food in Yugoslavia ranged between very good and very bad: "One day we arrived on location late and starving and they served us fried chains. When we got to our hotel room, mosquitoes as big as George Foreman were waiting for us. They were sitting in armchairs with their legs crossed."

After our reunion show a woman from the audience said, "I wonder what it would be like to be married to a man like that."

The late Anne Bancroft, who was, when asked a similar question had replied, "When he comes home at night and I hear his key in the lock I say to myself, 'Oh good! The party's about to begin.'"

How many of us can claim such a tribute?

SEPTEMBER 9, 2011

Tough Sell

"How does it feel to be Dick Cavett?"

That's what he said.

What a dumb question, I thought. This guy can't be very bright.

The "guy" was named Steve Jobs. Turned out he was reasonably bright.

The odd question was uttered in a posh New York restaurant a few decades ago. I'd been hired, or maybe was about to be hired pending Steve's approval, to do the first Apple commercials on television. He was a fan of my ABC show and had asked to meet me.

Herewith, a snippet from Wikipedia:

> Under Steve Hayden's leadership, Apple hired New York
> hipster talk show personality Dick Cavett as a spokesman
> and put Apple commercials on mass-audience television
> programming.

Hipster or not, I knew a fair amount about Steve Jobs and the mythic garage story. The garage in which young Steve and his friend Steve Wozniak put together not model airplanes but the prototype of what became that historic object, the Apple computer.

I was a little sorry Wozniak wasn't along that day because I'd read that he had lived in a tree. I'm partial to tree dwellers, having as a kid hoped to be one, when my little friend Bob Nelson (we were both little, of course) and I, out of sight of our parents, set to constructing a tree house.

We wanted ours to be as much as possible like Johnny Weiss-muller's arborial dwelling in the Tarzan movies we worshipped on Saturdays. Our carpentry skills were not advanced. What we ended up with, and had to settle for, was more of a tree platform.

The major-domo of the forgotten fancy restaurant may have taken Steve himself for a bit of a tree dweller. I can still see his caustic sneer of cold command—sizing up Steve full-length—at what may still be the only pair of jeans ever to inhabit those four elegant walls.

There was another man with Steve. Memory fails here, but I think it was most likely the great Jay Chiat of Chiat / Day; a jovial class act if there ever was one. In an aside to me he whispered, "Sorry about that question."

As with so many times in my life, I wish I'd kept some notes on the dinner conversation. In relative youth we assume we'll remember everything. Someone should urge the young to think otherwise.

Among the fragments I recall are a couple of Steve's wordings in his curiosity about how a talk show was put together. "How much do you go in with?" is how he put it. "How much is ad-lib? Partially ad-lib? Canned?"

He laughed when I objected to the word "canned" and suggested he rephrase it to "artfully prepared."

Interruption: In line with the French saying *l'appétit vient en mangeant* ("appetite comes while eating"), memories come back when writing. One minute ago, I didn't remember the following nice conversational exchange.

Knowing I was in the presence of genius, and thinking of the dopey edict of motivational positive-thinking charlatans that "you can do anything you want to do if you just put your mind to it," I wondered if maybe all brains are really alike. Could the right stimulus awaken previously dormant skills in us all? In other words, could I have invented the Apple computer?

It went this way:

D.C.: Mr. Jobs, from meeting me, does it seem possible that just the right cerebral spark in my head would have made it possible for *me* to have developed the Apple computer?

S.J.: I might have to know you a little longer.

(*Mirth ensues.*)

Un-self-forgivably, I failed to keep up our friendship from those days. Why do we do anything so dumb? (Or, if you don't, why do I?)

Our friendship did keep on for a time because I did do the commercials, and each time a new Apple model came out, Steve shipped me one. I'd put it in a closet.

After this had happened a few times, I got a call from Steve.

"Dick, a question. If I send you the next one, will you learn to use it?" (How did he know about the closet?)

"Sure," I said, wondering if I could. I think I suffered from the same ignorance that still keeps some people I know from getting one. The root word "compute" somehow suggests math, and that was always my scholastic downfall. I thought computers were really only for MIT types, not English majors.

Steve wised me up on that, sent me the new Macintosh—the white, upright one—and I loved it. In a note of thanks, I spelled the product's name wrong. Some English major.

Appalled, I called him to apologize. "Don't worry about it," he said. "You didn't spell it wrong. We did."

God, how I wish I'd kept in touch. So many subjects I'd love to have talked to him about, imminent death and how to deal with it not the least of them. Picturing Steve, I can still feel the intelligence that shone out from those eyes.

I had no experience with his reported dark, nasty, tyrannical side. To me he was one of the nice guys who—contrary to the old saying—finished first.

OCTOBER 21, 2011

Up Against the Wall

The scene is a freshman room at Yale, mid-fifties. Four occupants. First week of classes.

The dialogue:

"They must be kidding. We're supposed to go over to the gym and do *what?*"

"We all have to go over to the gym and have our pictures taken. Naked."

"C'mon. This isn't Princeton." (*Laughter.*)

"Are you serious about this? Is this April Fools' Day?"

Of course it was preposterous.

It was also true.

There were several things a Yale freshman was supposed to be able to do. You had to demonstrate in the Olympic-sized Yale pool that you could swim fifty yards or else be inducted into swimming class. (A sore memory: hearing, while panting, "You made it, Cavett, but if you fell in fifty-one yards from shore, you'd drown.")

Who'd have guessed that another requisite for being a true-blue Yalie was, strange as it seemed, good posture. Hence the phrase that yet lives in infamy, "the Posture Pictures."

Every single member of the freshman class in those days was required to strip for the prying camera. Then they put you up against a graph on the wall and photographed you, front, side, and back. Or as I put it years later in a comedy routine I did about this in my early

nightclub act—and in an appearance on the old *Merv Griffin Show*—
"You got three provocative poses."

In profile, the subject appeared to have a vertical row of needles
sticking out, up and down his spine. In fact, the needles were held
in place by adhesive tape and were "non-invasive." The needles had
something to do with the wall graph. There was, in this uncomfortable and decidedly unerotic adventure, no penetration. Mr. Cold
Hands, a man whose job it apparently was to affix the needles, pressed
the tapes firmly against your bare skin; a bit, I thought, too enthusi-
astically.

I remember—as a new comedian—killing 'em on the Griffin
show with this subject, and wish I could recall more of my admittedly exaggerated-for-comic-effect punch lines. But it almost doesn't
need any jokes.

One sequence I can recall went, "Some guys hated it; some
seemed to enjoy it. One guy tried to go through twice (*reasonable
laugh*); one guy fainted (*sizable laugh*); one guy tried to buy his pictures (*laugh*); and one guy tried to get his retouched (*boffo*)."

It was cold in there and I had somehow gotten next to last in line
in my group of embarrassed, mother-nekkid shiverers. Turning to
say "Wish me luck" to the last guy, behind me, I caused the poor
fellow to turn crimson. It was awful for both of us. I had caught him,
how to say, making an effort to present a more impressive image for
the camera. Blushing, he came up with, "There was some lint on it."

Should anyone think this bizarre undertaking was solely the
product of the mind of some demented old sod closeted somewhere
in the Yale administration, this coerced participation in a soft-porn
enterprise was intermural. And Ivy League–wide.

Of course, the screwball posture pictures practice has been long
discontinued, and years ago Harvard announced a total destruction
of its boxes of years of photos, as did other schools. And yet diligent
journalists have unearthed caches of them over time, still simmering out there.

Think of those who have risen to prominence in all fields whose sheepish full frontals are, many of them, still findable. Actors, judges, and presidents, husbands and wives of the prominent.

There are said to be collectors who claim to have prized specimens from the big women's schools. (Imagine "I'll trade you a Meryl Streep for a Hillary Clinton.")

People are shocked to learn that this was definitely not a boys-only phenomenon. Yes, the young "girls" (as they were still called back then) attending the finest women's colleges were told to drop their drapery and their drawers and exhibit themselves to the merciless lens.

Getting just a little serious for a moment, there are some astonishing facts here, one being: nobody protested. I never heard of a single case of anyone at any school saying they flatly refused to participate in this loony, outrageous, forced violation of individual privacy.

Somehow it isn't so surprising that guys played along. (A woman once asked me, "Is it true that men parade around naked in front of each other in locker rooms?" She said women didn't.)

Is it sexist to think this ordeal may have been more psychologically unpleasant, distressing—even damaging—for young women? Particularly those embarrassed by their less-than-ideal physiques? The awkwardly constructed and the obese?

According to someone who discovered a surviving cache of the racy pix of the young women of either Smith or Wellesley, many exhibit, by their expressions, combinations of acute discomfort, deep embarrassment, humiliation, and livid anger. But they "went along."

But surely not without troubling thoughts about who all gets the treat of ogling these, how many copies are made, what sort of security prevents prankish circulation—and what finally becomes of them.

I'm sure there are conclusions to be drawn here by deeper thinkers than I about obedience to authority, reluctance to rock boats with protest, etc. People hearing of this crazy caper on the part of major American universities say, "I wouldn't have stood for this for a second!"

If that's true, why did *everybody* go along back then? Were admissions committees' principles of selection inadvertently selecting the meek in vast numbers? Were "the times" so different? Woodstock, *Hair*, and countless plays and movies with the naughty bits on view were at least a decade in the future. Is that significant here?

Full disclosure department: I've never heard of anyone who saw his own picture. But I did. One of my roommates, Ron Wille, had the dubious honor of having as his scholarship job developing the damned things, and he sneaked me mine, temporarily. In it, I looked cowed. And there was about it a redolence of something greatly unpleasant, not immediately identified, having to do with the stark lighting (and the stark nakedness) and the chart and the pins that, combined, supplied a whiff of—not to get too melodramatic about it—the concentration camp.

Finally, doesn't all this vast embarrassment and fuss about a word you stop hearing as a third grader—"posture"—seem just a touch on the nutty side?

If you think so, you may have guessed it. There is another whole, hidden dimension to this story. The word "scandal" applies.

And "sinister" is not entirely inappropriate.

Stay tuned.

NOVEMBER 11, 2011

Last Nude Column (for Now, at Least)

Hey, thanks for the well-considered, enthusiastic, thoughtful, skillfully written responses to last time's "Posture Pictures" column.

And thanks to those who pointed out that the definitive master treatise on the touchy subject was written by Ron Rosenbaum in *The New York Times*. In 1995. (Glad my report was probably a new subject at least to my readers sixteen and under.)

Quite a few of you knew of Rosenbaum's piece—told in gripping detective-plot style as he tracks down the story, the dopey reasons behind it, and even a truckload of the allegedly long-destroyed salacious photos.

(Am I weird to wonder whether he found mine? Does Rosenbaum now know me better than I know him?)

The dangled and promised secret I tantalized you with in last time's column is thoroughly revealed by Rosenbaum.

Shockingly, the whole charade had nothing to do with posture.

It had to do, as some informed readers knew, with a man named Dr. William Sheldon (in sometime association with E. A. Hooton of Harvard) and his ability to somehow, back in the fifties, foist his screwball theories about body types and destiny on the highest levels of American academia. (Sheldon's infamous "somatotypes.")

Not insignificantly, it raises again the question of how our most vaunted educational institutions bought into his oddball theories wholesale and helped perpetrate them, containing, as they did, more than a hint of racism. (As in his assertion that Negro and Hispanic brains stop developing early.)

In a classroom a few blocks from the Yale gym where my class-mates and I were recorded mother-nekkid for the camera and pos-terity, I learned, in a psychology course, of Sheldon's now thoroughly laughed-off body type terms—"mesomorph" (muscular, fit), "ecto-morph" (skinny, cerebral), and "endomorph" (comfort-loving, tubby). (Crude translations are mine.)

Rosenbaum lays out how the mysterious acceptance of this theoretical crapola was bought wholesale by our highest houses of learning. The Yale professor George Hersey took the thing quite seriously, seeing it and writing about it as deeply sinister. He and others went so far as to connect the dread word "eugenics" to the whole mess, as well as the terms "breeding a master race" and, inevitably, "Nazi Germany."

Rosenbaum also recounts an incident involving me and the author of *The Beauty Myth*, Naomi Wolf. She informed *Times* readers that I, Cavett—as a guest speaker at her Yale graduation—turned the ceremonies into "the Graduation from Hell," destroying her (and every young Yale woman's) day by including in my talk the "posture pictures" bit from my old nightclub act, intending to show how Yale influenced my material as a comic.

With the Wolf sense of humor on hiatus, she said she was "shocked" (but clearly not speechless) at my saying that the Vassar posture pictures "were stolen [*reliable laugh*], ended up on the pornog-raphy market [*another*], and they didn't sell [*boffo*]."

(Wolf's tin-eared and decidedly vulgarized version of this could be entered in a botched quotation contest. Somehow she managed to get "New Haven's red-light district" into my act.)

Best of all, further venturing into fact bashing, she depicted me, at Yale, as George W. Bush's buddy (is this actionable?) "in an all-male secret society." (Yale had only males then.) I joined no society, secret or otherwise. And GWB and I were ten years—in many ways light-years—apart.

What ice does it cut, by the way, if privileged viewers of this ritual in nudity *were* the same sex? Reader Ann Drachman Tartaul writes of some discomforts of her experience, including: "Radcliffe College in 1948 required naked posture photos in the gym. The two gym instructors who were directing this project were lesbians. We all somehow knew this and were doubly humiliated."

(Lenny Bruce on that subject: "Gee, Miss Thompson's neat. She can throw a baseball just like a guy.")

Startling to hear from commenter "Thomas" that this was done to boys as young as thirteen at the, as he puts it, "once elite Hill School in Pottstown, Pa." This deserves particular condemnation because of boys' acute sensitivity about the unevenness of puberty ages. I can still see the sheepish looks and demeanor of the two guys in my junior high gym locker room, forced to undress and shower with all the other boys who had already (in my friend Ben's case, spectacularly) fully bloomed, shall we say.

Many asked the same question: Did anybody in the vast hordes ordered to strip protest? Or even question? So far it seems no one among thousands objected to this mandated humiliation.

How I wish I could report having asked at least "Why naked?"

Wouldn't it be just as easy to detect swayback, malformations, obesity, lordosis, and kyphosis in both sexes while clad in their undies?

It's always hard to wind up a column so that it doesn't seem to just stop. Let's let a reader inspire today's last word, a reader with a provocative thought and who apparently prefers to be known only as "SS":

> Did the posture researchers aim specifically for the private schools, the Ivies, the places where they thought America's future leaders would be found? There's a subtle, twisted notion to play with!

Thanks, "SS," for allowing me to concoct the following fantasy: "Dear Presidential Candidate Bush: I have in my possession . . ."

DECEMBER 2, 2011

Deck the Halls with Boughs of Nutty

You may see this as a companion to my last year's bittersweet Christmas entry. Some found that one a bit too poignant.

I envy, in a way, those who continue right through adulthood to just love Christmas—the way we did as kids, beaming at the thought of festooning the tree with tinsel, hanging the capacious stocking (faintly redolent of mothballs), and hoping Santa had gotten all our hints, and, if you're old enough, cursing those damned strings of lights on the tree where if one burned out they all went out and you had to seek, one by one, the dead culprit. (How easy we have it today.)

In my case, some affection for the hallowed time has returned markedly, after at least twenty Christmases spent on Virgin Gorda, British Virgin Islands, happily far from the familiar list of horrors that are part and parcel of Noël in Gotham, my favorite city.

To call New York's traffic at holiday time a nightmare is to understate. And, incidentally, was the Christmas tree at Rockefeller Center dreamed up by a sadist? The presence of that bloody conifer helps achieve gridlock for acres in every direction. That lovely, unoffending tree, from its peaceful forest life untimely ripp'd.

"Dumbos from New Jersey," as a cop once told me, seem to think they can pile the family into the car, drive right up beside the big spruce, and pull off a few souvenir needles—learning the hard way that it's probably easier to edge the car up to the White House and tap on the occupants' windows. So, while disappointed kiddies squall, the parents discover they're lucky to find a parking place from which they can't actually see their house. As for the sidewalk mobs of loutish, pushy shoppers, these offer the less-than-jolly dangers of pickpockets, transmitted flu, and the possibility of a rib-cracking crush.

I have, by way of contrast, lovely memories of many standard Midwestern Christmases in Nebraska, with happy families and jovial visitors and strung popcorn and peanut brittle and snoozing dogs by the hearth. You felt warm and protected, surrounded at a full dining room table by relatives who, before dessert, swore they'd begin their diets the next day and who stayed on for canasta or Monopoly.

One salty memory comes back. Every year, my German grandmother insisted that my father place prominently on the tree a faded and ancient glass ornament from her earliest childhood memories in "the old country." It must have belonged to generations of the Pinsch (her family name) clan since before Germany began starting wars.

It was a delicate and remarkably unattractive twisted glass cornucopia, about five inches long. At its lower end, the opening of this horn of plenty, the partially faded colors of its fruits and vegetables were still fairly bright. One year, my dad seized the thing and barked, "Do we have to look at this damn thing every year?" Startled, "Grossmom" asked why he would say such a thing about her beloved treasure.

"Because it's ugly. It looks like a goose with a bouquet in its fanny."

(*Exit Grossmom in tears.*)

Many years pass. Through an odd set of circumstances including sudden unemployment as a writer in Hollywood, owing to the cancellation by ABC of the imploded *Jerry Lewis Show* of 1963—a television mishap sometimes accidentally misfiled in archives between the Hindenburg catastrophe and the *Titanic*'s descent from view—I found myself, with five other people, the only passengers on a full-sized airliner on Christmas Day—the best day to fly. We were bound from that less significant coast to this one. Where New York is.

I was yet a bachelor and, still freshly a New Yorker, living solo in the city of my dreams, partaking hungrily of all the advantages from cultural to carnal thereof. (The former outran the latter, by a mile.)

My Christmas feast that year: a lone, late lunch at the Automat.

Here's the setting: I was closely flanked, at tables left and right, by two diners, each unaware of the other.

To my left, a lumpish geek, munching and dribbling. Don't ask me why I imagined his first name to be either "Gort" or "Lunk." I went with "Lunk." His grubby costume was topped—as it so often is in such cases—by the thick, droopy earflap cap favored by the lumpish gentry. His teeth? Grounds for a dental hygienist to switch careers.

His counterpart, the female of the species, resembling in face and costume one of the trio of "weyard sisters" who perform the opening number—"Double, double toil and trouble"—in a traditional production of *Macbeth*. I dubbed her "Gravel Gertie." Her costume featured mismatched galoshes.

Near each other, but at adjoining tables, they were in their own individual worlds.

I was able to hear them both—mantra-like mumblings with similar but separate themes. Both stared into the middle distance. The day's subject: an analysis of the city's troubles. Brief samples will do:

Lunk: "It's the hook-noses that's to blame. The hook-noses got all the money. The mayor's a prize one if I ever seen one." (He was referring to Robert Ferdinand Wagner. Of the R.C. Church.)

G. Gertie: "It's the black ones causin' all the trouble. Look at that one over there. Look how they eat with their hands."

I looked and saw a nattily attired gent, dining solo. He was consuming not a handheld slab of zebra meat, as her words might have suggested, but instead—and she was right about the manual part—a small cinnamon roll.

Both now lowered their volume and for a time proceeded to issue, in unison, a kind of unseasonal contrapuntal chant from which assorted varied and creative ethnic slurs emerged like grace notes.

Arising to go, I got their attention and, to the amusement of some people at a nearby table, uttered what seemed an appropriate question.

"Why don't you two get married?"

They blinked opaquely, and I bade adieu to Christmas at the Automat and stepped out onto Lexington Avenue. A pretty snow had begun to fall, and because of it, a sweet thing happened.

The sublime final paragraph of James Joyce's "The Dead" began to play in my head—the bits I could remember—about the snow that "was general all over Ireland . . . softly falling into the dark mutinous Shannon waves falling faintly through the universe upon all the living and the dead."

Healing snow.

I pictured the pair, after they had ceased to dine, and wiped their mouths—or failed to—heading for their respective lairs. That gentle snow would, without prejudice, descend on Lunk and Gertie. Softly and silently, in the season of brotherly love.

DECEMBER 23, 2011

Marlene on the Phone

It was a bitter cold day on the end of Long Island. I was not alone out there; my two dogs and I had come in from a hike in the woods at the exact instant that the phone rang.

A friend of mine who can "do voices" the way Darrell Hammond can would sometimes delight in fooling me, calling in a voice duplicating that of the then-not-late Walter Brennan, or Raymond Burr, or a cartoon character, or a contemporary singer, male or female. Once it was an impeccable Dudley Do-Right.

This time it was Marlene Dietrich. I was a little cold and irritable and came back with, "And I'm Frank Sinatra. What can I do for ya, Marlene, baby?"

As you may have guessed, it was not my lucky day. Or, at least, my lucky moment. The caller was indeed Marlene Dietrich.

The room swayed a little as the throaty and infectious laugh, somehow both amused and forgiving, delighted the ear, making apology unnecessary.

We had never met.

Our connection was her daughter, the beauteous Maria Riva, who in the Golden Age of TV seemed to be the most employed actress on the tube: *Playhouse 90, Studio One, Kraft Television Theatre*, all of them.

She had played the Shubert Theater in New Haven in *Tea and Sympathy* when I was at Yale. At my instigation, my roommates and I cornered her at the stage door and invited her to visit Yale the next day, and she did, nearly knocking dead a fellow student who dropped in, saw her seated on our (cruddy) couch, and gulped "Well, *hello!*" while catching his balance.

But that's another story. This is about "Shanghai Lily" herself.

I still hold out hope of finding my long-lost notes from these conversations, because this was not to be the only call from Dietrich. They were loaded with gems, but I was about forty, which we now are told is when memory starts dropping things overboard. If my accursed sloppiness and disorganization haven't claimed still another treasure not taken care of in an adult manner (I'd hoped psychoanalysis might cure this), maybe one day I can give you more delicious details now floating in the "limited access" section of the memory bank.

Anyway, here's one: As we chatted along, suddenly she asked, "What can you see from where you are right now?" What an original question. Never been asked that before or since. "Two things," I said, and then told her: the Atlantic Ocean and a paperback screenplay of my all-time favorite movie, *The Third Man.*

"The one with Orson on the cover, holding a gun?"

It was. She asked whether I could see his nose. Before I could say that of course I could, Miss D. asserted in a sly tone, "No, you can't. No moviegoer ever has. Orson has always been ashamed of his little tipped-up baby nose. Like Larry Olivier, he has a different nose in every movie." Sure enough, he had a good, sturdy nose in the picture.

Glad to have this bit of insider knowledge from one gargantuan star about another, I decided to be just a slight bit daring: "I suppose you two were, at the very least, great, great friends."

She managed to extend her wonderful laugh all through the sentence: "Mr. Cavett, what are you hinting at? And on what you might call our first date?" (I won't even try to describe the fantasy-making potency of that remark.)

Not sure my blush wasn't audible, and before I could stammer something, she went on: "That could never happen, Orson never made even a mild pass at me. I was a little insulted until I realized the problem."

(Was she about to deliver some startling revelation about Orson Welles's sexuality? The answer was yes.)

"Orson could never be attracted to a woman"—here she wickedly paused—"who was a blonde. Never. Look at his girlfriends. Spanish, Italian, Indian, Rita—" (If you have to ask who "Rita" was, you probably don't belong here.)

She went on: "Then, what do you think happened? We made *Touch of Evil* and he made me up very dark and they dyed my hair black. After all that indifference, I was suddenly the dark apple of Orson's eye. After all that time, overnight, it was suddenly, 'I have to have you.' I had to lock my dressing room door."

Impertinently, I asked, "While he was outside it, or inside?"

She rewarded me with the great laugh and accused me of "dangerous wickedness." Her tone was flirting. I ate it up.

For the next three days the phone rang at the stroke of 10 a.m. (German efficiency?) and we resumed. I'm trying not to get icky about this, but each time that famous voice began to sound, I learned the meaning of the phrase "a heady presence." It filled the room.

Between talks #3 and #4, she bought the book *Cavett* and read it overnight. For the fourth call, instead of "Hello" I got "You are to eat up." "Excuse me?" I said, hoping to hear it again, which I did. She said she loved the book (and by implication, me?) and could not put it down till the end.

If it had been dark, I would have glowed.

Her daughter wrote a deeply satisfying—and startlingly frank—book about her mother ("about her mom" doesn't sound right for the Blue Angel). Yet she was a devoted mother and a doting grandmother, sometimes spotted, babushka-concealed, pushing a baby buggy in Central Park.

A sincere tip: move heaven if not earth to see *Marlene*, Maximilian Schell's great Oscar-nominated documentary about Dietrich.

It was shot in the Paris apartment in which she had sometime earlier holed up and in which—having allowed virtually no one to see her for years—she died at ninety in 1992. You only hear her voice, in Schell's brilliant interviews. I doubt that there's a better documentary about a legend. A must if there ever was one.

I could happily have talked to her every day for a year. Finally I asked when we could meet.

"Oh, dear. I'm too shy for that," she joked mock-girlishly and changed the subject.

She loved language, spoke several, and haunted late-night bookstores. Literacy was a must. I told her about a journalist who, when I used the word "profound," said, "Ooh, *profound*—I'm going to have to look that up."

"Oh, God, no!"

During World War II she was the most intrepid of troop entertainers, and not just in safe areas. Endearing herself to a generation of soldiers, she slogged with them through mud in Germany and Italy. She saw more combat than many soldiers, maybe even more than Dick Cheney, Newt Gingrich, and George W. Bush managed to avoid. (Perhaps a trio to include in a "Monument to the Well-Known Dodger.")

She was raised a Protestant, but the war took her faith away. "After the horrors I saw and the preachers on both sides praying to destroy the other side, I refuse to believe those I loved and lost are floating around up there somewhere. If God exists, he needs to review his plan."

Amen.

Of course I wanted to ask about a few of her best-known affairs: James Stewart, Jean Gabin, John Wayne, George Bernard Shaw (dubiously), and, less dubiously, John F. Kennedy. The story goes—this from a high-placed source—that after their initial encounter, JFK asked, "Did my dad really have an affair with you?"

The scrupulously honest Miss Dietrich said no; to which the leader of the free world replied, with characteristic gusto, "I knew the son-of-a-bitch was lying!"

Because she was a participant in and product of the sexually versatile *Cabaret* Berlin of the twenties, I would love to have gotten to know her well enough to get her to talk about that time. (To be fair to both sides, her affairs included the notorious Mercedes de Acosta, Garbo's girlfriend.)

Alas, the calls and our "relationship" came to an end as suddenly as they had begun. Sometimes it seems it was all a dream. (Yes, I sat by the phone a couple of times more.) And it just hit me that at least one of those chats might survive, on an old answering machine tape, a machine that sometimes failed to shut off when talk began. Anyone out there good at searching? Come on over.

JANUARY 13, 2012

Should News Come with a Warning Label?

We're told that anger is good for you. Getting it all out and all that.

But we're also told the opposite is true. That worry, stress, and gut-grinding anger produce and lay down in the body injurious plaques and acids and biles that can and should worry you and your insurance company.

So with all the shocking, ghastly items reported in recent days—soccer goons brawling and leaving scores of people dead; a policeman shot in the head, and the accused gunman cocky and smirking in custody; truck drivers who (although copious Red Bull swiggers) still manage to nod off, committing human mayhem; the supposedly respectable teacher accused of having covered kids with cockroaches, molested them, and recorded his handiwork with his camera; and on and, yes, I'm afraid, on.

Let's agree to forget an NBC game show (*Fear Factor*) in which contestants—eager for their fifteen minutes—were induced to drink donkey semen. Lest it be accused of poor taste, the network spared us the airing of it. (Should they be required to reveal who thought of the idea?)

Surely such punishing news is hazardous to your health. Should newspapers, like cigarettes, be required to carry a printed health warning?

I'm wondering whether I cling to certain things that anger longer than other people do. The mere name Dick Cheney, for instance, still does something measurable to my pulse rate. He whose "priorities," as he put it, didn't happen to include his own military service. In his and his war-inflicting boss's eyes, serving was, as the phrase goes, for other people.

Why do such out-of-the-past items still get to me, starting those harmful juices flowing, in some cases decades later? Why can't I, oysterlike, cover the Cheney irritant with the magic fluid that that remarkable shellfish coats his painful grain of sand with?

And what, of all the recent stories to get mad about, have my ulcer-making bodily substances chosen to fasten upon?

Vassar.

In case you missed it, this august institution managed last week to break the hearts of dozens of would-be students eager to study there.

If there were a contest for devising an action that would emotionally crush a large, large number of innocent, unsuspecting kids, Vassar's "error" might just take the prize. Let's look at what they did.

They informed a large number of applicants to the freshman class that they—with Vassar's congratulations—had been accepted.

Sheer joy.

And then—after screams of delight and friends' congratulations, after champagne corks had popped, elated relatives had been informed and, who knows, perhaps clothes shopping was contemplated—there came a second message.

Sorry, we were wrong.

I don't doubt they're sorry. But couldn't they have done a little better than hide behind what's become the modern blunderer's favorite cowardly refuge, "computing error"?

Computing error? Nice to know that no humans erred at Vassar. A head might roll.

Parents have reported heartbreak and sadness. At least one student almost catastrophically canceled her other applications. Thanks to Vassar's incompetence, kids looking forward to the adventure of freshman year may now, if something doesn't go right in the spring, spend it turning beef at McDonald's.

One heart-deprived columnist wrote that "life is unfair" and that while the episode was "a bummer" it was "not the end of the world"—and that kids as a result might learn something about life. She recommended a "this, too, shall pass" approach.

It'll pass! Same to you, lady, when you get your kidney stone!

You, too, may wonder why I'm so worked up over this. It's because I can identify. I recall opening with trembling fingers the letter from Yale that would surely tell me politely that it was not to be, but thanks.

My mind's eye can still see the very typeface of the word "Congratulations."

I can't even imagine what a Vassar-like follow-up—"Whoops. Sorry"—would have done to me.

Finally, I admit with some difficulty that I'm sorry for Vassar. It can't be pleasant for so distinguished an institution of learning to take such a squalid pratfall in public. And we're told constructive criticism is always better than carping. So how about:

1. Set a splendid example for the world. Admit those kids whose emotions you've trampled on. At half tuition.

2. Or, help them get into another school and pay for some of it.

Unrealistic? I suppose so. But surely all those fine Vassar minds combined can think of something better than *Too bad*.

I love the statement in *The New York Times* by a young victim who said that maybe it's for the best, that she had dreamed of going to Vassar to major in computer science but that "Vassar doesn't even know how to use a computer on the biggest day of our lives."

Is it vile of me to hope the talk of possible lawsuits isn't idle?

I hope Jane Fonda cancels her alumnae donations over this.

FEBRUARY 3, 2012

Schooling Santorum

Truth be told, I'd planned on a lighthearted topic for today.

But in line with last time's subject—the deleterious effect the news can have on your health—those threats to the blood pressure continue with no shortage of headache and stomach-acid-stirring topics to jostle our wellness, if not our actuarial tables. A few minutes of CNN this morning did it.

Just about any pair of random news items is enough to make you reach for the Bisodol. Today's two: the stupidity of the Koran burning by American military personnel and our baffling, cowering impotence in the face of Bashar al-Assad's bloody slaughter, in Syria, of man, woman, and child—victims apparently not as worthy of our caring, or of life, as their counterparts were in Libya. You can get ill from this.

And there's still Rick Santorum, alas. As Joan Rivers might say, *"Please!!"*

We learn from him that contraception is a sin. Giving birth (sorry) to the possibly rude question of how the Santori as a couple and as obedient Catholics managed to have *only* eight children over all those years if they didn't, well . . . never mind.

Remember the "rhythm" method, humorously called "Vatican Roulette"? A friend of mine says he knows full well that he and his sister "owe our existence to it." An apt name, roulette being the worst-odds sucker game in the casino: *Let's do it, dear. The odds are only 37 to 1 against us.*

Maybe they cheated now and then. The thought might not have

arisen were I not typing this shortly after one of the most soundly defeated incumbent senators in recent history spent part of his time at the—one dearly hopes—final "debate" reeling off the number of times he was forced to vote contrary to his beliefs!

We're taught in early schooldays by our wise teachers and kindly parents that it is not nice to comment on or make fun of people's appearance. But does Santorum look like a president?

Not that you have to be of majestic aspect, I suppose, but he's really pushing it. When you think of Lincoln or FDR, to name but two, Santorum in comparison looks like someone who'd play a character called Ricky in a mildly amusing sitcom.

Try to picture Rick's countenance Photoshopped into that famous picture from World War II, sitting in Roosevelt's place, side by side with Stalin and Churchill in Yalta. It would look like two redwoods and a spirea bush. Is that bland Santorum visage suitable for Mount Rushmore? *That* would look like the Great Four and Pee-wee Herman.

The sweater vests don't help.

My soul similarly rolls over and groans whenever Santorum uses the phrase "homeschooling." I first heard about it in the dim days when the John Birch Society was a going thing. (Young folks, I don't blame you for not believing that this organization held that President Dwight Eisenhower was a "conscious, dedicated agent" of the Soviet Union.) Some benighted McCarthy-admiring parents decided to pluck their children from the clutches of "commies" teaching our kiddies their godless doctrine.

I have lost track of distant relatives of mine, parents who also snatched their young kids from school and, for their remaining school years, stuffed them mainly with the Bible. (I'd love to know how they did on their SATs.)

I feel sorry for the poor kids whose parents feel they're qualified to teach them at home. Of course, some parents are smarter than some teachers, but in the main I see homeschooling as misguided foolishness.

Teaching is an art and a profession requiring years of training. Where did the idea come from that anybody can do it? How many parents can intuit how to do it? (Pardon unconscious rhyme there.) My parents were teachers, and the thought of homeschooling sent them rolling *before* they were in their graves. Especially when parents, complaining of their kids' schooling, wrote in report card responses things like "I am loathe to critacize"; "my childs consantration"; "normalicy"; "my daughter's abillaties"; "her examatian grades"; "she should of done better"; "greater supervizion," etc., into the night.

To deny kids the adventure and socialization of going to school, thereby missing out on the activities, gossip, projects, dances, teams, friendships, and social skills developed—to deny kids this is shortsighted and cruel. I think of the mournful homeschool kid watching his friends board the school bus, laughing, gossiping, and enjoying all that vital socialization we call schooldays.

Besides, aren't you arguably a better person for having *gone to* school rather than having had it funneled into you by dreary old Ma or Pa in their faded bathrobes at home?

And what is the argument for it? For some, is it to protect their innocent ones from hearing words like, oh, *sex* and *contraception*? From forced association with those less desirable ethnically? Maybe it's to keep them safe from radical notions like the idea that fossils and carbon dating aren't put there by the Devil to fool the scientists, but prove the world has billions, not thousands, of years on it.

Surely, there are parents caught in mediocre school districts with little choice but to give their kids the best shot at a rounded exposure to arts, letters, the sciences, and so on, and are admirably able to do so at home—thereby sparing them the *teachers* who can't spell and who tell the kids, as in one friend's case, that the band around the center of the earth on the globe is called "the equation."

Who knows what sorts of fears haunt the minds of homeschooling parents? I guess it's always possible, when Sally or Billy is walking to school, that a dark figure might leap out of the shrubbery, maniacally shrieking, "There's climate change!"

Again, teaching takes skill and education and dedication. Home-schooling as an idea is on a par with home dentistry.

FEBRUARY 24, 2012

Road to Ruin

More and more as the years dissolve, every time I get behind the wheel I think how remarkable it is that anyone who drives, or rides—or in New York City, walks—is alive.

Rarely do I, at the moment of ignition, fail to hear in my mind's ear the voice of old Ben Washburn, the mechanic from my childhood in Nebraska, recite his mantra for me as I watched him work on wrecks. In those insane days before seat belts, he'd always point out the cannonball-sized hole on the passenger side where the unlucky head went through the windshield.

His mantra: "Every time you get into a goddamn car you're a-enterin' a death machine." In a more expansive mood, he might add, "Either your death or somebody else's." If that second line came, then so did, with a little dramatic nudge in the voice, "I've seen it too many damn times."

As a young kid (as distinct from all those old and decrepit kids, I guess that phrase means), I'd encountered more than my share of ghastly blood-and-brains-all-over-the-highway traffic accident aftermaths.

We've all seen, or been in, or narrowly averted a deadly accident. And had those assorted little chilling moments of "Whew! I failed to look left . . . but got away with it this time."

Still, I'll bet you haven't been through the following frightful happening. If you think you have, I probably will have told it wrong.

Somewhere in the eighties (the twentieth century's, not mine) I was home from New York in Lincoln, Nebraska, and I borrowed my parents' car to go for an extended spin. My father, a worrying soul about my driving wisdom, pointed out that the weather was a bit dicey, flirting with thirty-two degrees. I assured him I hadn't lost my driving skills by living in New York City and knew how to turn into a skid, etc. (I didn't admit that I *liked* to skid on icy roads and frequently did so when no one was around, entertaining myself with my skid-and-spin-stopping prowess.)

Just short of my goal, Grand Island, where we used to live, I decided to make a side trip to a beloved Western historical museum in the town of Hastings. I remembered it fondly, having bought treasured, real arrowheads there as a kid—from five cents for a bird-point up to twenty-five cents for a handsome spear-point, all gleaned from the surrounding and magical Nebraska prairies.

About ten miles short of Hastings, rolling along nicely in a light, cold rain—on that dangerous invention, a two-lane highway—it happened.

As I was passing another car at a moderate forty-five m.p.h. or so, my windshield wipers stopped working. They didn't stop going back and forth; they just stopped removing the drops. Puzzled at how the blades of *two* windshield wipers could have worn out at the exact same time, I "heard" my father's voice, as I always do when passing another car to this day: "Get the hell around 'em!" Obeying by adding a little gas, I noticed that, although accelerating, I wasn't passing the car I was allegedly passing.

From this point on, everything took on the quality of a dream—the kind where you can't get any traction.

What had a moment earlier been big raindrops on the wind-shield, which were instantly swept away by the wipers, were now nickel-sized globs of what looked like library paste. And they were sticking in place. The wipers made a distinct scraping sound rubbing over them.

And now a bread truck coming my way, without slowing, flew off the road and slammed into a ditch, sending the driver's head forward with an appalling bounce. Just then, my father did another cameo appearance in my head. "Whatever you do, for God's sake don't ever get caught in"—and here came the bone-chilling phrase—"*freezing rain!*"

I had.

I guess I had always thought that freezing rain was another way of saying hail. Or maybe sleet. How dumb.

The reason I wasn't passing the other car was that the world had turned to glass. Wet glass. I remembered in a flash a bonus question on a ninth-grade science test in Mrs. Gloye's class: "It would be desirable to eliminate all friction from the world. Yes. No." If, upon reading this, anything resembling thought flitted across my brain just then, it must have been, "Yeah, things wouldn't wear out." I got it wrong.

Now I saw how wrong.

The total loss of friction is unimaginable and nightmarish. Everything in the world—cars, telephone poles, electric lines, grass, the highway, the signs, a dead raccoon—looked glass-coated and gleamed like diamonds. The car I had tried to pass made a half circle and went sideways off the road, missed me by so little that I waited for the crunch, and smacked into a telephone pole. The whole thing cast a glaring light on the stupidity of my answer to Mrs. Gloye's friction question.

Again I could hear A. B. Cavett's voice from way back, probably to my mother, admonishing, "If freezing rain ever happens to you, for God's sake keep your foot off the brake—don't touch it—and let the car come to a stop."

Thanks to this, I guess, I was the only car still on the road. Everybody else must have reflexively hit the brake. But no one seemed to need treatment, and I decided to try for Grand Island.

Somehow I got the car turned around in what must have been a hundred itty-bitty back-and-forths, virtually in place. Crossing the Platte River bridge, normally the work of a minute, took about a half hour of gently touching the gas, sliding slowly into the rail, bumping it, turning the wheel a bit, sliding and bumping the rail again . . . for what seemed like a week.

Eventually creeping into Grand Island, I urged the car into a parking space on the main street. The rain had only just begun to freeze there, providing no end of sadistic entertainment.

In what a writing teacher might mark "Unlikely exaggeration!" everybody who came out of a store fell down.

When a four-way light changed, those getting the green continued. So, to their surprise, did those getting the red. Half a dozen cars were sucked into a cluster at the intersection with a sickening timpani of booms, thumps, and crunches.

In the ensuing days, Grand Island's fender repairmen must have earned retirement to Florida.

I remember feeling sorry for the victims, and at the same time sorry for everybody who wasn't there to enjoy the free comic spectacle of all those helpless bumper cars and spectacular Buster Keaton pratfalls.

Shamefully observing, sitting snug inside your car, you'd catch yourself going: "I hope that pompous, stuffy-looking guy coming out of the dime store . . . Yup! There he goes!" (So far as I know, no one reduced the comedy quotient through lethal injury.)

To my surprise, despite the front-row seat to the tumble derby, I had fallen asleep, sitting there in the car. The numbing tension and concentration required to urge the car along the face of the ice-coated bridge and roads of Nebraska at a barely detectable speed for what had felt like hours had taken their toll.

When I awoke, a slight rise in the temperature had resolved the beastly situation. The dream had ended and the world was merely wet again.

For a long time after this I was spooked about getting behind the wheel under anything but a sunny sky with a cloudless horizon.

That sudden utter loss of control was bad-dream material happening in waking life. It was akin to suddenly going blind or becoming paralyzed. A vital element of the life and the world you knew was suddenly gone. Control was gone. You were plunged from normal existence into helplessness. Anything you did made things worse.

That summer I'd been in a production of *Richard III* (Shake-speare's, of course, as distinct from, say, Soupy Sales's *Richard III*), and a line from it sounded in my head the next morning. All night the darkest aspects of the experience had replayed themselves in fitful dreams. And in that way of dreams, the psychic pain was somehow worse than in the actual events. The bard's line that sounded was, "I would not spend another such a night / Though 'twere to buy a world of happy days."

Nor another such a day.

What can we learn from this? What's the moral here? Just this. If you ever get caught in this bad-dream situation with that ogre from hell, *Freezing Rain*, when the wipers stop removing the drops,

(a) Take your foot off the gas.

(b) Hope it *is* a dream.

MARCH 16, 2012

Groucho Lives! (In Two Places)

For the Groucho Marx fans of this column who continue to plead for more, the information contained herein, if new to you, might just make your day.

There are two very different books out, both of which are musts to grace the bookshelves of the Groucho addict: Robert Bader's *Groucho Marx and Other Short Stories and Tall Tales: Selected Writings of Groucho Marx* and Steve Stoliar's *Raised Eyebrows: My Years Inside Groucho's House*.

Those who may have read these books when they first appeared need not feel left out. Both are updated and expanded editions. Both contain abundant new stuff.

Woody Allen has said that of the greats, Groucho had the richest number of gifts. He could sing, dance, and act, and beyond those fairly common gifts, when you add the distinctive voice, faultless instinct for wording, genius wit, hilarious physical movement, rich supply of expressions, and physical "takes"—and the list goes on—it arguably adds up to the most supremely gifted comedian of our time.

And there's one thing more. He could write. A born scribe. And many a Groucho fan is unaware of the degree to which this was true.

This problem has been put to bed by Bader's book. (Full disclosure: I know Rob from the masterful job he did putting together the *Dick Cavett Show* DVD sets.) Bader, too, can write, and in a fresh, humorous, scholarly, and entertaining way, with shrewd analysis and observations about the products of Groucho's pen and type-writer.

If your reaction to this is "So what did he write?" this book holds the answer. In his early years, and aside from his books, Groucho's written pieces appeared widely, including in the beloved magazine *College Humor* and, yes, *The New Yorker*. Bader has found and retrieved priceless specimens of Groucho's impressively large output from all over, some of the pieces early enough to have been bylined "Julius H. Marx," Groucho's *vrai nom*. Open the book to any page and try not to laugh.

Prime among the delights for me are speeches Groucho gave at colleges and elsewhere through the years. As you read them, it's almost like having him present. So tone-perfect are these pieces that you can't help hearing the famous voice and its witty inflections in your mind's ear. It's a wonder.

A Marx Brothers fanatic virtually from birth, Bader is an intrepid researcher and gets stuff nobody's got. For another, coming book, he can be found one day in the Lincoln Center Library or, on another, in local newspaper files in, say, Red Oak, Iowa, sleuthing out yellow-ing local Marx Brothers clippings, reviews, and material from their vaudeville days.

Groucho preferred the company of writers to that of actors. In Los Angeles, when he took me to the Hillcrest Country Club for lunch, he steered us past a table of beckoning movie faces to the writers' table, where I met fabled "names" from a lifetime of reading screen credits. He told me once, "I'd rather be known as an author and remembered for my writing than for all the rest of it." (He told others that, too, of course.) He was immensely proud of having been a houseguest of his pen pal T. S. Eliot. The only problem, he said, was that Eliot kept addressing Groucho's then wife, Eden, as "Mrs. Groucho."

Groucho was a well-read, well-educated man (the "self-" method) and the only ninth-grade dropout I ever met who had read all of Iris

Murdoch's novels. I think he was quietly delighted when I, with my (envied) Yale degree, had to confess to having read not one.

Steve Stoliar, while still college-aged, was part of the successful campaign to force the 1974 rerelease of *Animal Crackers*, the Marxes' 1930 film, then inexplicably in mothballs and in danger of being lost, deteriorated, and forgotten. This brought him to Groucho's attention. Sufficiently impressed by Steve's knowledge of the world of Marx, Groucho offered him a job and he "woke up" inside his hero's house, transformed from mere fan into archivist, general amanuensis, and companion to his personal god. A dream that he hadn't dared to dream had come true. How many of us can say that?

Raised Eyebrows is an invigorating read. A gulping Stoliar got used to opening the front door to a who's who of the arts and letters: S. J. Perelman, Bob Hope, Steve Allen, Morrie Ryskind, Jack Lemmon, George Burns, and many more cherished friends.

Guests, after dinner, were treated to a cabaret with their host by the piano singing, with perfect pitch, "Lydia, the Tattooed Lady," "Father's Day," "Show Me a Rose," "Omaha, Nebraska (in the Foothills of Tennessee)," and other favorites, often with Marvin Hamlisch volunteering at the keyboard.

Raised Eyebrows could easily have been written as a delightful memoir only. It is that, but much more. There's no way Stoliar could have avoided dealing with the rhino in the room: the enigmatic, half-mad Erin Fleming, the young woman who came into Groucho's life at a crucial time and who became, in a complex and bizarre way, his Lady Macbeth. As you'll see, she was equally adept at doing wondrous things for Groucho, and appalling ones.

Depending on whom you ask, she was either the best or worst thing that could have happened to the aging star, who provided her a pass into a world of fame and the big time that she could never have otherwise achieved. In my view, she was both: the worst and the best. Young and pretty and vivacious when Groucho met her, Erin and her ambition worked—some would say wormed—their way into his home and she became, in effect, his life manager. Her story as told by Stoliar is the stuff of one swell hair-raising novel or movie.

On the plus side, she got Groucho up and out of near despair at a time when he was feeling forgotten. (A woman who lived near Groucho described how, in a deeply lonely period of his life following a divorce, he would walk his dog in front of his neighbors' homes, hoping, she said, to be invited in for a drink, a visit, or a meal. That gets to me.)

Another paradox about Groucho was the contrast between his claim to be shocked by the dirty talk and material of the 1960s and '70s and his own propensity for the hilarious filthy remark.

"I don't belong in this age," he said once on my show, where he also discussed the Broadway musical *Hair* and its then shocking nudity. "I was going to go buy a ticket," Groucho said, "but I went back to my hotel room, took off my clothes, looked at myself in the mirror, and saved eight dollars." (He'd have saved a lot more today.) Would-be comedy writers: note the perfect ad-lib wording, syllable count, and cadence.

Bader did some bowdlerizing of Groucho's stuff in the original edition of his book, and has kicked himself for it. In the interval he decided to restore everything, feeling it was not his duty to deny the reader Groucho unadulterated. (Congratulate me for not using the phrase "letting it all hang out.")

Stoliar's update on Erin Fleming revisits the old question about whether she eventually attained the state of genuine madness. Long-memoried viewers of Ted Koppel's *Nightline*, on the very night the verdict in the crazy *Erin Fleming v. Bank of America* trial came down against her (there is much to Google on this case), would not need a degree in psychiatry to diagnose what appeared to be someone certifiably unhinged. Imagine the lack of charm and appeal it would take to cause a jury to decide *against* a young woman, in favor of so revered an institution as a *bank*! At one point, viewers of news coverage of the trial got to see Fleming point across the courtroom and shriek at a Bank of America attorney, "That man murdered Groucho Marx!"

Stoliar's update section also includes some fascinating information about Erin's mystery-enshrouded demise.

The truth is, Marx devotees will need to get both books. And if you're not a devotee, get them anyway. Fix a drink, light a fire (I won't add "only if you have a fireplace"), put one book on each side of you, and dip alternately. There are so many worse ways you could spend your time.

Trying as usual to think of how to close this off—a problem Groucho never had in his letters—I remembered an example. He once ended:

Well, Richard (I'd say "Dick" but my secretary is a spinster), I'm running out of things to say. And they should be running out of me.

Anyway, good-bye 'til hell freezes over. And if you've read this far, there's something wrong with you.

Groucho

MARCH 30, 2012

They Dressed Like Groucho

You could say, with partial plagiarism: *It was the best of nights. It was the worst of nights.*

I remember thinking that it might be a long time before I saw so many happy people in one place. The place was Carnegie Hall and the people were fans—worshippers might be the more appropriate word—of Groucho Marx.

At least half the eager throng was a young, college-type crowd; it was at the peak of the time when the Marx Brothers—and I, to some extent—were campus heroes. The controversial (mildly put) Erin Fleming (see previous column), the young woman who was running Groucho's life and household for both good and ill—had hauled the frail fellow out into public once more.

To the dismay of friends and relatives, who feared that in these sadly waning years, Groucho, with formidable powers decreasing noticeably, lacked the stamina, let alone the desire, to perform again, Erin had lined up a series of "concerts," the true purpose of which many felt was less to get Groucho back in the limelight than to get Fleming into it with him.

There were two fears. Would he be physically able to get through a full-length concert, enfeebled as he was most days then, and what would it do to him if only a handful of people showed up? Could he survive that? That latter fear proved unfounded.

When the big night came, I had the cabdriver let me off out front, instead of at the stage door, to assess the crowd.

There was a touching aspect to the milling, chatting, laughing throng. Some carried pictures of Groucho and his siblings, some had painted on Groucho mustaches. Hurrying back to the stage door I must have seen at least a dozen fully-got-up Grouchos complete with swallowtail coat. There were even a few Harpos and Chicos. (I saw no Zeppos.) Nice kids in a troubled time.

It was 1972—not a nice time in the country—and there was something so sweet about these kids that I couldn't manage to ditch the thought that some equally nice kids might have loved to be there but for their having been, just two years earlier, shot dead by the National Guard at Kent State.

Pushing dark thoughts aside, I went inside and up to the dressing room. I recall now that the words and melody of Groucho's friend Harry Ruby's "Everyone Says I Love You" began to play in my head in Groucho's voice, sung by him on my show a few years earlier. This was going to be a great evening.

I entered the dressing room and was horrified. Groucho was slumped on a couch looking more frail and papery than I had ever seen him. The famous voice was a hoarse whisper. I thought of those milling kids outside in a near frenzy to see their hero and here he (all but) lay before me, looking like moribundity warmed over. Clearly it would be a miracle if we could get him downstairs and to the stage, let alone through a two-hour concert.

"How do you feel, Grouch?" I asked with forced brightness.

"Tired."

And then: "Did I ever tell you about the time George Kaufman . . ." It was an anecdote he'd told me at least four times. Not a good sign.

I went over to Erin, energetically finishing her makeup, and said, "What are we going to do?"

"He'll be fine," she said cheerily and, undaunted, went on with last-minute preparations. Was this blindness? Madness? Or was it something else? It reminded me, somehow, of one of those performances that heroic mothers of dying children are able to summon, bustling about with a chipper air and saying with a smile, "Today, we're going to read a lovely story."

I couldn't decide if Erin was crazy or I was. The music in my head—in that weird way the mind has of selecting appropriate music—had switched to the theme from *The Blue Angel*. It crossed my mind to thwart Erin by whisking Groucho up and out a side exit and putting him to bed. But I figured both she and the audience would hunt me down and lynch me in Central Park. Instead—and although no one's ever explained *why* it must—the show went on.

I remember going up a few steps and onto the famous stage in front of the great curtain, to a bombardment of cheering and applause. Was this all for me, I humbly thought, or because I was clearly the instrument by which they would soon see Groucho? I managed to convince myself it was some of each.

(A side note: I recently re-found a letter in which Groucho thanks me for my services that night and adds, "The record people are crazy about your introduction and want to use it on the record. I'll look into it. I expect they'll be owing you some payment." If that was true, it still is.)

Back to our story. Scanning the packed house from the stage and spotting Woody Allen and Diane Keaton in aisle seats, I launched into the introduction of "a few people that should be mentioned."

"Among them: Rufus T. Firefly (*explosion of applause*), J. Cheever Loophole (*again*)—hold your applause to the end, please—Dr. Hugo Z. Hackenbush, Otis B. Driftwood, Captain Jeffrey Spaulding . . . and the one, the only, Groucho."

The join in the curtain moved a little and Groucho shuffled forward.

The place went wild. A truly moving hero's welcome. The rafters, and your eardrums, seemed threatened by the bellowing, stomping, whistling, clapping, and unbridled cheering. You could see people laughing already to the point of tears.

His performance consisted mostly of an unenergetic reading of his favorite anecdotes from three-by-five cards; a thing I feared might turn even that audience to stone.

But a sort of miracle took place. They were so pre-sold to have the time of their lives that they barely seemed to notice any difference between the all-but-drained Groucho onstage and the capering madman of the movies. And, as an actor still susceptible to a booming audience, mercifully he did "come up" a lot.

Still worried and thanking the gods that we got to intermission, I went back and suggested cutting an energetic musical number between Groucho and Erin in the second act in order to conserve the old man's energy.

Erin—already costumed for the number—gave me a look that brought to mind the chilling close-up of Laurence Olivier as Richard III, looking down at the tart-tongued little child prince he will soon murder. I backed off, retaining my status as perhaps the only person in her life she never had harsh words with. And maybe she knew best. Somehow those gods, and she, got us this far and through the rest of the evening—and in fact, as it turned out, many more.

I was told later that a small mob of the kids, including some of the costumed ones, who couldn't get into the sold-out hall, simply hung around outside, seemingly content to be at the same place where their hero was. And some got the treat, cheering, of seeing him get into the limo at the stage door.

The evening also provided, for me, one of what I call "through the looking glass" incidents. It could also be called "How did I, specifically, get here?" It's kind of corny to talk about it, and some doubt the genuineness of the feeling as merely an opportunity to drop a name or two. It's the feeling of: How did I ever manage to get from being a kid seeing Groucho on the screen of the Grand movie theater in Grand Island, Nebraska, to now being in the backseat of a long black car with him? (If you know, please provide the answer.)

After all these years, I still don't know exactly what I feel about all this. I'm so close to the forest as to be almost one of the trees. Yet it seems that whatever manipulations and self-promotions and hectoring Erin may have been guilty of, she did bring a good measure of light and cheer into Groucho's last years.

At his house in Beverly Hills, she frequently stage-managed dinner parties with his cronies and admirers. She fed him straight lines, she set up anecdotes by bringing out awards and letters and mementos from the famous; and around dessert time, when he became restless, she got him to the piano to regale everybody with Harry Ruby songs, or the Gilbert and Sullivan numbers for which he had such a passion. Doubtless overtaxing him at times, but also putting him where he loved to be: on, and the center of attention.

I once heard Henry Kissinger say about Richard Nixon something like "Just about anything you could say about him would be true." So of Erin. For better or worse, she brought a near-dead man back to life repeatedly, even if she seemed to risk killing him in the process.

And very near the end, he was still able to bring his own light and cheer. Visiting a friend in the hospital, an exhausting chore at his age, he was able to say, as the elevator door closed, "Men's tonsils, please."

Steve Stoliar (author of *Raised Eyebrows*) reports that near the end, when vital signs were low, a nurse entered Groucho's bedroom with a thermometer.

"What do you want?"

"We have to see if you have a temperature, Mr. Marx."

"Don't be silly," said the barely audible figure in the bed. "Everybody has a temperature."

It may have been his last joke.

Despite everything, despite his reported crankiness and even cruelties in his unhappy times with his children and wives, I hope some kind of peace is being enjoyed by the man who merits our eternal gratitude for having lived in our time; who imagined the Stamp Act of 1765 as two fellows who came onstage, stamped their feet, and finished with a song; or who could say to an operator, as I heard him do, "Extension 4-8-2, eh? 4-8-2. Sounds like a cannibal story."

Such a man deserves flights of angels to sing him to his rest. Let's hope, for his sake, they sang something from *The Mikado*.

APRIL 20, 2012

Pyramid Power, Over Me

Dick Clark's death reminded me of how much a part he was of some of the most fun I ever had in my life. I mean being on *The $25,000 Pyramid*.

Password was fun, too, and being a panelist on the old *What's My Line?* was a superthrill. But the laughs gotten from my friendly sparring with Dick Clark were great, and the games themselves were a day at the gym for your brain. Five shows in a row taped with only economics-dictated short breaks between them left you all but cortex-dead and, when the show was in Los Angeles, barely qualified to drive yourself home.

I liked Dick Clark and we had a pleasant, kidding on-air relationship that played well, and it was fun winning money for the civilian contestants. Although I had never been a fan of *American Bandstand*, I had admired his defiance on that show of the "too many black ones" crowd who threatened his sponsors. He and I had an odd thing in common: people on the street frequently said to him, "Hey, aren't you Dick—um—Cavett?" And I got the reverse. (Once it was, "Don't try denyin' you're Dick Clark." I didn't.) And whenever we saw each other, we'd compare how many times this had happened to each of us since the last time we'd met.

The show was still in New York the first time I did it. My ABC show had ended, and eerily, the *Pyramid* set was in my old studio in place of mine.

In those days *Pyramid* was on only once a week, in the evening, and they taped two at once. I'd never seen the show and somewhat foolishly accepted the offer. Not the move of a wise person, but it turned out okay.

Recklessly, I learned the game on the job, so to speak. Dumb as this was, it was also good in a way. I had nothing to lose, didn't even care whether I won or lost, and this relaxed me to such a degree that in the two tapings, I—and my partners, of course—beat the pyramid all four times, costing the company a bundle.

Somehow I was invited back, and having learned how chancy and nerve-racking the whole thing actually was, I tensed some and, caring now, I with my perfect record began to lose sometimes, like everybody else. What can we learn from this?

Here is a sample of the self-inflicted but pleasant torture of pyramiding.

The host's and my on-camera "feuding" was lighthearted, and Clark's perfect combination of a quick mind, genial on-camera nature, and masterful ability to hit just the right note in banter made him perfect for his job.

A sample of our allegedly humorous joshing:

He'd say, "Our next contestant comes all the way from Florida and—yes, what is it, Dick?"

Me: "If she hadn't come 'all the way,' she wouldn't be here, would she?"

He would deftly and expertly express mild exasperation and move briskly on.

A very few experiences on the show were less than fun.

Memory just coughed this up. A woman I was teamed with got eliminated in the first round when I, seeing the easy clue "aspirin" and with just seconds left, apparently went nuts and said "acetyl-salicylic acid." Unforgivable. Was I showing off? Why not just say, in succession, "pill" and then "headache." Anyone breathing would have replied "aspirin." As she was led from the set, she turned for what was usually the inevitable moment of, *Oh, well, it was nice meeting you, Mr. Cavett.*

Her version: "Thanks a lot! I needed the money."

I still ache from this. I owe her a check. I wish I could find her.

A job on that show that I would not have wanted at (almost) any price was the one held by the poor fellow who, watching from the control booth, had to make—under inhuman pressure—the instant on-air decisions about what answers and clues to accept or reject. (Was "calm" acceptable for "relaxed"? "Grasp" for "grab"? Etc.) All the while knowing that his snap decisions might please or infuriate his employer, and delight or break the heart of the civilian contestant. A job, I should think, that would make air traffic controlling look simple.

Yet he was a cordial fellow, pleasant of appearance and quite thin, probably from difficulty with keeping solid food down. I hope that in retirement he has found some degree of well-deserved tranquillity, perhaps in a rest home in a pleasant setting by the sea. And without ever, ever again having to decide in a flash if "amble" and "stroll" are the same thing.

One of Dick's and my running humor gambits was my joking questioning of some of those decisions. It was harmless, quick, and fun, and caused no trouble. And nobody got hurt. Until one day.

First, a kind of secret was revealed in confidence to me by a staff member I'd become friendly with. I assume the statute of limitations is not a factor here, but I shall not identify him further.

Early on, after doing the show a few times, I noticed that the last subject as you climbed—the top square of the pyramid—was harder to convey than the rest. Considerably harder. It was more abstract, or something. Where the bottom rows might have been easy stuff like CHRISTMAS THINGS or BURT REYNOLDS MOVIES, a top square, just as things were going swimmingly, could suddenly bring your brain to a halt. It was like going from, say, U.S. PRESIDENTS to THINGS THAT CHANGE. Or THINGS THAT HAVE ENDS. What would you say to those, instantly and unambiguously, with time running out? (Once I got THINGS THAT PENETRATE. I'd give a lot to know if I said the obvious one.) The staff member confided to me, in a lowered voice, "Around the office, we call the clue in the top box 'the money-saving clue.'"

It's a triumphant memory, though one not without pain. A contestant and I—and I'd love to find her—were doing fine. We'd won the first round at the desk and thus were promoted to the big pyramid, where the big money lay.

We got through the two lower rows of subjects without much trouble, as I recall, and had plenty of time for the "M-n-y S-v-ng Clue."

It turned around and the mind reeled.

THINGS YOU BIND.

"The nation's wounds" didn't occur until years later. Nothing occurred at all.

I'd recently held a fishing pole and noticed the lacquered "binding" on the handle, so I said "fishing pole handles." And was immediately sorry.

"Things you hold," ventured the contestant.

"Uhh, books," I tried.

"Things you read. Things with paper. Rectangular things."

Not surprisingly, my next clue, "magazines," didn't convey the bound sets in my mind.

I tried another: "A sprained ankle."

"Things that hurt, painful things."

Time would be up in three seconds at most. I don't actually remember thinking—in any sense of the word "thinking"—this, but my mouth, along with some unconscious recess of the brain, blurted out, "Chinese women's feet."

"Things you *bind*?" (*Pandemonium.*)

Moments like that were glorious. The cheering, the jumping up and down. The jubilant, celebratory, spontaneous joy. The intimate, automatic close-body embrace with the contestant, of either sex, bordered on the erotic. One of life's great moments; or at least so it seemed. Maybe that night, trying to get to sleep, you didn't torture yourself by wishing that, in a blown game that day, you hadn't said "handcuffs" instead of "cuff links."

But, in its own category, there occurred the Fateful Day.

A female contestant and I were climbing smoothly toward the pinnacle and the big bread. And then it happened.

The deadly top box turned around, revealing: THINGS THAT HAVE PITS.

Me: Coal mines.

Contestant: Things that are dark. Deep things.

Me: Cherries . . . uh, plums, plums and peaches.

Contestant: Fruits. Things that are round. Things that are sweet. Things with juice.

Me (*feebly*): Peaches, cherries.

Contestant: Juicy things. Things on trees.

I thought of, and rejected, "the human arm," and suspected that "tooth-breaking fruits" might have too many words. Though probably, sadly, not.

Although I doubt that the phrase "think outside the box" had been born, it's what I tried, in a panic. The gleaming "$25,000" sign glared at me: the amount that the woman was clearly not going to win in the remaining few seconds. Then, from where I know not, It Hit.

Me: Poe's pendulum.

Contestant: Things that have *pits*! (*Crowd explodes.*)

Joy all around. Then tragedy. Dick Clark, looking pained and reluctant, announced that his earphones had just conveyed the news from the booth that the upright judge had rejected my clue. Hissing and booing filled the theater.

I blew. "What earthly reason could anyone with half a brain—and it would take half a brain—come up with for rejecting that clue?"

(*Audience cheers.*)

Clark (*listening to earphones and a little sheepish*): "They say that Poe's pendulum doesn't have a pit."

Me: "*What?* Every schoolkid knows it's 'The Pit and the Pendulum.' It's not 'The Pit and the Cabbage Leaf' or 'The Pit and the Subway Token.' It's 'The Pit and the Pendulum.' Did you ever see Poe's pendulum without its pit? What kind of reasoning? You get an intelligent audience here. Why don't we let them decide this one? Is 'Poe's pendulum' fair?"

(*Massive roaring and approval out front.*)

I like to think I was angry on the contestant's behalf and not about the rejection of my clue.

I don't remember at what point they had to stop the tape. Since the shows were timed precisely to the second to avoid editing costs, which I had now incurred for them, plus overtime pay for crew, etc., for the one-after-the-other, five-shows-a-day schedule—you went half brain-dead somewhere in the fourth one—they weren't happy. I was marginally less than *persona grata*.

Alas, they stuck with their wrongheaded decision. And saved money. It still gets to me as I type this. I wonder if I thought of paying the woman myself?

I'd love to see that show. I missed it on air, and I can't imagine how much of it, with challenging editing, they managed to air to make it presentable. But there's more.

About a year passed, and I was back on *Pyramid* again. In the parking lot, one of the show's staff, looking cautiously both left and right, said, "We were wrong about 'Poe's pendulum.'"

I wondered, did they contact the contestant? His chuckle answered that question. If she's reading this now, she has, at least, the dubious reward of knowing she won.

In spirit.

I still wish the show would come back.

MAY 11, 2012

You Gave Away Your Babies?

"Didn't you just hate giving your jokes away and seeing some-one else get the laughs?"

It's a common question to comedy writers. I still get it. And the answer is no. At least I didn't, and my colleagues didn't, and I could never figure out why people assumed gag writers for famous come-dians felt like Cinderellas.

Or that they lurked enviously in the dark shadows of the wings—as their boss got laughs—filled with envy and dreams of usurping the crown.

Statistically, I'd say comedy writers are perhaps the sanest cat-egory of show people. And why not? They make *big* money, and although it's not an easy trade—particularly when you're at your galley oar five days a week—it's easier on the nerves and the psyche than living with the brain-squeezing pressure and cares of being the Star.

You don't have to pay a press agent, or if you choose, not even an agent. (My great friend, the late sitcom writer David Lloyd, saw no virtue in paying someone for years—10 percent of your earnings—for having made perhaps one phone call. David composed his own contract. Its short opening paragraph: *Mr. Lloyd will not, at any time, be either asked or required to be associated in any manner, shape, or form with "Laverne and Shirley."*

Other advantages of writer versus star: you can dress sloppy, work mostly at home, not obsess over your aging face, hair, and body, not get sued or bugged by camera wielders and tabloids and cranks who claim you stole their ideas, and not have your sex life and divorce displayed publicly in a variety of decorator colors. And you never have to risk flopping onto your butt, or face—or on bad nights, both—in front of an audience. That list of advantages could go on and on. And, surprising as it may seem, I never knew a staff comedy writer who yearned to be the Star.

As one writer put it, "Jack, Johnny, Jerry, Milton, they're nervous wrecks from morn till dusk, wondering how long they'll last. The only fun they have in life is the minutes they're actually out there doing the show. [*Painfully true of Johnny, I'm afraid.*] I go home without a care and enjoy my house, my family, my lawn, and my dog. And my lack of even a single ulcer."

He might have added that he's not plagued, while at the top, with disbelief at how high he's climbed and nagging fears about just how long that precarious status and all that fairy gold will last.

People have assumed I was the exception. "Every time Jack or Johnny or Groucho or Jerry Lewis got a laugh with your line you died a little, right?"

The truth is I felt elated, fulfilled, successful, and thrilled that a huge star had just said what I wrote. I never dreamed of being the host of a show. My highest ambition in that regard was to maybe, someday, somehow, be a guest on a talk show. Even just once. (Talking about what? I hadn't worked that out.)

Years later, blessed and saddled with my own show and the pressures, pleasures, and pains thereof, I admit I would now and then recall a good line I'd written for others and wistfully admit that it would have been fun to get that particular booming laugh myself.

Example: The buxom beauty Jayne Mansfield was at the peak of her movie fame, and my boss Jack Paar was beside himself with the thrill of her appearance. On the day, he lined up the writing staff in his office and said her introduction had to be "extra special." The five of us went back to our Remingtons and tapped out flowery compositions attesting to Miss Mansfield's looks, talents, and knockout physique and presented our offerings to the boss.

Jack wadded them up.

In my mind's ear I can still hear our combined product hitting the dread wastebasket at Jack's feet. And the assertion that we weren't trying and hadn't given him but scraps of material he could use in weeks. That was Jack.

Irked, I suggested in the hall that we all go get our carbons of the good stuff of ours he'd used in those "weeks," but wiser, older heads prevailed.

We took another shot at our assignment of producing an introduction worthy of Miss Mansfield and her outstanding (sorry) attributes. And failed again.

Two of the older veteran writers, insulted, were on the verge of just going home. As the nonveteran kid on the staff, I was afraid that Jack's snit bore just the hint of a mass firing.

So, not feeling the same job security Jack's longtime writers enjoyed, I tried once more. Fired up by the mission of perhaps saving our collective arses, I typed briefly and quickly, ran down and dropped it on Jack's desk and hurried away. He liked it. It's only a little immodest to haul out the cliché, but it did all but stop the show.

Paar: "Ladies and gentlemen, what can I say about my next guest, except—Here they are, Jayne Mansfield."

The line enjoyed a measure of fame, and once or twice it was accorded the honor of having its authorship claimed by others.

There were other such instances. If I had been the sort who suffered over giving his babies away, it might have been over a product of my brain that was in a category I don't know the proper name for—"overweight spoonerized *jeux de mots*," perhaps.

For instance:

The Tonight Show in the sixties. The front page of that day's *New York Times* bore a large photo of crowds at the Met viewing Rembrandt's famous painting *Aristotle Contemplating the Bust of Homer*. ("Bust" seems to be the theme here.) It had sold for some fantastic seven-figure sum, and people were well aware of it from the massive publicity. Jack was off that night, and Hugh Downs was subbing. Hugh, an educated, literate man with a fondness for humor and wordplay, seemed the right person to either delight with—or fob off on—the odd, misshapen creature my strange brain had given birth to. I felt Jack probably would not have chosen it. Hugh did.

As Hugh presented it:

> I often wonder who thinks up those sometimes amusing captions under news pictures in the paper. Just for fun, pretend your job is to come up with a caption for a certain photo that's going to appear in tomorrow's paper.
>
> It shows the world-famous billionaire Onassis out in Hollywood, standing in front of a house he's thinking about buying; a house that once belonged to a famous silent screen star named Keaton. I wonder if the right caption might be:
>
> "Aristotle Contemplating the Home of Buster."

Whenever I've seen Hugh in years since, he'll recall it and laugh. This oddball gag went 'round the world. I'm told there were attempts to translate it into other languages, which is hilarious.

Imagine the heads scratched in France, Germany, or Japan, trying to figure out in Cherbourg what's funny about "la maison de Buster"; in Bremerhaven, "das Haus Busters"; or, in Yokohama, "Basutaru-san no homu."

Learn English, folks!

JUNE 8, 2012

Vamping with Nora

So frequently the wrong people die.

While traveling in a remote part of western Nebraska—away from the news media except for little local papers—I saw a friend's e-mail suddenly change from its harmless subject to the appended line, "Sad about Nora Ephron."

One of those moments when the mind does its inadequate best to fend off the truth. *"What's* sad about Nora? Surely not—"

We sat, facing each other, dismay bordering on panic. The setting: *The Dick Cavett Show,* somewhere in the early seventies. Nora and I are talking. My producer, sheet-white, had just delivered the news during a commercial that my next guest, a famously eccentric genius actor with a legendary thirst, had, in a gesture of professional shabbiness, gotten "tired" of waiting backstage and had left. (His initials are Nicol Williamson.)

Nora and I, having used up all our good stuff and at the point where I was supposed to say "My next guest . . . ," now faced what felt like a Sahara-wide *half hour* of remaining airtime to fill. We set forth on our trek.

It may sound improbable that two such, ahem, engrossing people couldn't fill the time as if tumbling from a log. At this distance, it seems crazy to me, too. But it's a peculiarity of such a show that it somehow doesn't work that way. We had, in the elegant phrase, shot our wad. I wish I could make that convincingly clear. It's a little like asking a singer or dancer, wiping their brow after having successfully done the expected performance they were geared for, to do two or three more right now just like it. The mind has moved on. It's weird and shows again how just "sitting and talking" on TV is not remotely like doing the same thing in real life.

After what seemed like an hour of gasping for air, lurches and restarts and awful pauses, we had killed only ten minutes. Only twenty to go.

Each time I looked at the studio clock it seemed to show the same time it had before. Had the hands been welded in place? In a state of stunned disbelief we somehow dragged ourselves, and what felt like at least two tacklers—and any remaining viewers—to the goal line. As the closing theme song mercifully sneaked in and the eon-length show faded from the screen, we, at least figuratively and maybe in fact, fell into each other's arms like two survivors pulled from a mine.

And agreed to meet the next day to plot the slow death by poison of Nicol Williamson.

Years later, Nora pointed out that at all our subsequent encounters, before cordial greetings, each gave a little involuntary shudder upon seeing the other. Like friends who'd survived a long-ago car crash together.

All that aside, I did one good thing for Nora and her arsenal of talents. I gave her a play to write.

It had to do with the notorious incident on my PBS show when I had lightheartedly asked Mary McCarthy, who'd talked about underpraised writers, to name some *over*rated writers.

That's when she delivered her famous remark about Lillian Hellman that "every word she writes is a lie, including 'and' and 'the.'" It flowered into a notorious lawsuit about which much has been written. Including a Broadway play Nora managed to construct from the wreckage.

In the world of letters it was generally held that by suing, Hellman had disgraced herself and betrayed her own principles about free speech and criticism. Nora saw Hellman's actions as "a kind of dance of death." An effort to, in fact, shorten McCarthy's life; which, in my opinion, the anguish and costs of Hellman's monumental lawsuit undoubtedly did. (It amused Nora that the late Pulitzer Prize–winning writer and my hard-drinking friend Jean Stafford always referred to Lillian as "Old Scaly Bird.")

But that same Nora found the appallingly spiteful Hellman to be a vastly entertaining friend who made her laugh. She called her, in a chat we did for the now defunct magazine *Show People*, "too much fun to hate."

In that same staged restaurant "conversation," Nora told me she was startled to read in her morning paper just what in fact had happened the night before on the Cavett program.

"One of the rare nights when you missed my show, Nora?" I asked.

"One of the rare nights when I missed your show," came the reply, with a wry line reading that Eve Arden might have envied.

Intrigued and inspired, Nora turned all this unwieldy and psychologically complex matter into an entertaining play, *Imaginary Friends*. The long-standing hatred between these two competitive women who became famous at the same time (1929) had all the seeds of drama. Nora stated at our magazine interview lunch what could hardly be called a trivial factor: "They had a lot to fight about. One was beautiful and one was not."

I told Nora, in a merry jest, that I had tried out for the part of "Dick Cavett" in her play but had been turned down.

"We wanted someone younger." (*Laughter all around.*)

I loved making Nora laugh out loud. We talked about Hellman's *Julia*, a tale apparently bogus from tip to toe. In it, Lillian claimed to have risked her life during a dangerous period in Germany by smuggling a vast number of German marks—hidden in her hat—to Julia.

I said that owing to the value of the mark at that particular time in Deutschland, to have smuggled, chapeau-wise, the amount Lillian claimed, her hat would have had to be the size of a Volkswagen. Nora's laugh was my reward.

For Nora at her deadliest best, I recall a review she wrote in *The*

New York Times in 1972 of three books about and by gossip columnists. One of the books was the columnist Sheilah Graham's memoir about her sex life. Its title—and could you have guessed?—was *A
State of Heat*. Nora wrote, "I'm afraid I may have made 'A State of
Heat' sound like one of those 'so-bad-it's-good' things. I don't mean
to. It's as close to being unpublishable as anything can be these days.
Sheilah Graham has been in on a pass for years as a result of her
affair with Fitzgerald: it's about time it ran out."

I don't know how to close this. If there is that so-called better
place, then Nora's surely in it.

Her going left ours a lesser one.

JUNE 29, 2012

Comedy Pain and Comedy Pleasure

I guess this could be called Part 2 of an earlier column, which was inspired by readers asking me to talk about comics and comedy writing. So here's more.

Let me take you back to Ed Sullivan days and start with that which was part of the life of a New York–based scuffling comedy writer of the time: the phenomenon of the B-level comedian.

Not the beginner or the guy who entertains at picnics and church socials, but a professional comedian who is *sort of* in the big time without being of it. He works reasonably steadily in nightclubs and the borscht circuit, has had a few TV "shots," and has a modest house in Queens or Brooklyn. He is, as the saying goes, on his way. Eternally.

I can't forget my first job working briefly for a prototype B-level comedian, now gone, at least from the scene.

In his career, he had achieved that maddening level of what you could call semi-recognition. On the street, he would get, "Hey, ain't you, uh—? Don't tell me . . . uh— The guy from Ed Sullivan, uh—" (The comic reveals his name.) "Yeah, that's right! I reconized yuh." (A certain stratum of New York street society drops the g in "recognize." So does the increasingly rare English-speaking cabbie.)

I've been there. You have to be on TV a surprisingly long time before you're stopped on the street. Then, when you are, you get a lot of "Hey, you're great! What's your name again?" (It happens not only at the beginning of careers, but . . .)

The comic that, as Jerry Lewis likes to say, "I have reference to" illustrates a sad aspect of that life. A dream comes true. He's lucky enough to get career-making Ed Sullivan appearances, to do well enough on them, and yet still toss at night with a sour stomach, plagued with the lifelong inability to figure out why he never "moves up." Up there. With Benny, Hope, Marx, Burns, Berle, et al.

I once asked my shrewdly perceptive former manager, the legendary Jack Rollins—who handled the careers of comics big and small—what separates the frustrated medium-timers, even those who are by no means bad, from the big-timers.

Jack thought a bit and said, "When they ask me why they can't reach the top, I really don't know what to tell them. Or even myself. The only way I can think to put it is what I'd call a certain lack of *largeness* in them."

My guy had a particular style and vocabulary and way of phrasing things. I'd seen him and I could imitate him at the typewriter; the *sine qua non* of being able to write for a comedian.

The late Mort Lachman, long Bob Hope's head writer, explained to me, as a relative kid in the business, how that's the trick. He said you can write for a famous comedian only if you can turn him on in your head: "You have to hear their voice and their inflections as you type, and hear the difference between how Benny would say it and how Hope would say it." (For younger readers, substitute Stewart and Colbert.) He advised that "if they sound all alike to you, be a plumber. You'll make more money."

I could do what Mort described with Comic X, referred to above. Upon my first laying my jokes in front of him, he uttered, in my presence, a classic line. And I only am escaped alone to tell thee.

I handed him some pages of good (trust me) material, and as he finished reading and I assumed a modest expression, awaiting my compliment, he removed his glasses, held my gaze for a disconcerting moment, and uttered a statement that deserves immortality.

Instead of praise, I got, "This isn't comedy material. This sounds like stuff I'd say."

With a little help from me, the remark made its way like wild-fire through the world of comedy writers.

And now an item seemingly from the supernatural.

When TV and Sullivan came along, it was both a great and a tough time for purveyors of stand-up humor. Typically, comics who'd done their reliable act for years in vaudeville and hundreds of clubs got one shot on Sullivan, rejoiced, and then got invited back. Yikes! What to do? Naturally, they had used (blown) the best stuff from their acts the first time. Stuff they'd made a living on for years in vaudeville and clubs.

I had a one-time job with one of these desperate souls.

I can still hear his anguished phone voice pestering me at all hours. "Ya gotta help me, Dick. I'm layin' off here"—read "out of work"—"and I've got a Sullivan shot."

I wrote him some new stuff. I needed his modest stipend. So, with a headache, and with both my heart and Aspergum in my mouth, I went with him to the live Sullivan broadcast. One of the theater's twin gods smiled on, let's say "Georgie," and he did well.

A particular one of my lines worked beautifully. He was a "zany." Part of his shtick, was, while talking, to suddenly duck and swat at imaginary insects attacking him. It was funny, but it needed a big new laugh. I wrote, *Grab the bug out of the air, smash it in your hand, hold it up, and say to it, "Aha! Thought the mustache would fool me, didn't you?"* It brought down the Sullivan theater.

I went backstage to congratulate him and for my pat on the back. I should have learned by now. I got: "Dick, when you write for me you gotta give me more than just one great line!"

Another line for the books. Soon, our paths diverged.

The opposite could happen. The personally lovable, hilarious "insult" comedian Jack E. Leonard hosted *The Tonight Show* a few times in the interim guest-host summer between Jack and Johnny. "Fat Jack" always used his favorite insult line, "Why don't you put your glasses on backwards and walk into yourself?"

I thought he might like a variation and gave him "Why don't

you walk into a parking meter and violate yourself?" He used it, and it, as they say, killed. He thanked me for it each and every time I ran into dear Jack for the rest of his life.

And, I just remembered, he never forgot another line of mine. Hugh Downs, Jack Paar's Ed McMahon, sat nightly next to the host. Hugh had been dubbed "an intellectual." I gave Jack E. the line, "It's hard to concentrate with Hugh Downs sitting here humming a crossword puzzle." I have to admit being surprised that this got such a blockbuster laugh. (But not surprised that I would mention it here.)

All of this returns to the question: What is it about the comics who see no difference between their limited talents and those of the giants? I'm always amused by the witless complaint I can recall hearing even as a kid and as recently as a week ago: "Why don't these old-timers move over and let somebody else have a chance?"

As if there were only a certain number of places at the "top"— like limited seating on a bus—until somebody gets off. As if until some top star retires or expires, no aspirant can move into the newly vacated spot.

Now for what I once heard called in an ad agency meeting "an added plus." An incident I find to be almost spooky, with a touch of synchronicity, perhaps. See what you think. It's a comedy collector's item. A curious accident leads to a great joke and a huge laugh.

It took place as I sat alongside Jack Benny on my mid-seventies ABC late-night show. An odd thing happened at the very end of our conversation.

This is hard to make clear. As Jack and I chatted, something put the idea of Jack Benny and life insurance into my head.

I've decided I must have had, just below the level of conscious-ness, a memory of some Jack Benny joke on that subject. But only the idea that there may have been such a joke, way back somewhere. I also remember thinking, as we continued to chat, that it was an ideal subject for a Jack Benny joke.

The fun here was that when I said "life insurance," it stirred some-thing in the Benny head—but not yet the joke. I saw him noodle and fill verbally for a moment as if sensing that something was there. And then, *click*. Jack's memory retrieval released the joke and Jack, delighted, fired out the line with a smashing delivery:

> J.B.: Then I go to Chicago, because I have business. You know, I'm with the American Republic Life Insurance Company. And there's a very dear friend of mine who owns it, Watson Powell. And I meet with him and we talk some more business . . .
> D.C.: Are you a business associate or are you covered by them?
> J.B.: No, I'm not covered by them at all, I just work for them.
> D.C.: But you have life insurance.
> J.B.: Have I got life insurance? My God, I could go into a routine about that.
> D.C.: Well, you don't need to—
> J.B.: I'll tell you the kind of life insurance I got: When *I* go, *they* go!
> (*Pandemonium.*)

It's so strange. Just before the joke burst into life, neither of us had it in his head. At least not the conscious head.

The best part for me was Jack's visible delight in having excavated from memory a great joke from his past. And the *very* best part was that as the segment faded out, he shook my hand to thank me for the "setup" that gave him, and us, a gigantic laugh.

I just loved it.

Sitting there with that great comic artist, I might well have thought, "Toto, we aren't in 'This sounds like stuff I'd say' land anymore."

August 3, 2012

The Fine Mess Maker at Home

"Fat and skinny guys comin'!"

That's how a Nebraska playmate of mine would burble the news that if Saturday would ever come, we'd be once again rolling with laughter at Stan and Ollie. Twice. We'd learned how not to get caught, sitting through for the second showing.

If someone had told me then that I would one day meet a member of that beloved team, my mind would have had no way of processing the thought.

I'd be as likely to meet Donald Duck.

Just out of school and working as a copyboy at *Time*, I returned a folder to the "L" section of a file shelf and noticed the next folder said, "Laurel, Stan." It was 1960. Who knew he was alive?

Fade down and back up.

I was a writer now with Jack Paar and the show was in Los Angeles for two weeks. A note to Mr. Laurel had gotten an immediate response, self-typed, beginning with an almost courtly, "Dear Dick Cavett, Thank you for your letter, containing such kind sentiments, so graciously expressed." Also within was a postcard-sized photo of Laurel & Hardy (beside his smiling face he had penned, "Hi, Dick!")—and an invitation to visit him in Santa Monica. (Where, unbelievably, he was in the phone book!)

It came to pass. For maybe the first time in my life I was ready, dressed, and combed an hour before it was time to go.

I drove slowly to Santa Monica and the Oceana Apartments,

facing the sea. There on the side of the building was the same logo as on Laurel's apartment stationery. This somehow confirmed that, far from dreaming, I actually was about to meet the man who helped the fat man struggle and wrestle and heave that piano up that long flight of steps in *The Music Box*.

Inside. The desk.

"Mr. Laurel, please."

A dreary, bored clerk, without looking up: "204, up those stairs."

He didn't seem part of the magic.

I took a breath, rang, the door opened, and my not having met Stan Laurel abruptly ended.

"Well, lad, it certainly is nice to meet you."

There he stood. No derby. No silly grin. No shrill, squeaky crying of "I didn't mean it, Ollie . . ." Just a nice-looking gent in a white shirt and tie and a warm, welcoming manner. The face was fuller, but the eyes—and the ears—were instantly familiar.

But there was one thing to certify who it was. The slight speech impediment. The familiar Laurel fricative on the *s* sound. (Webster: *fricative: frictional passage of the expired breath through a narrowing at some point in the vocal tract.*) Every impersonator of Laurel, including me, does it. I spared him my version.

On people who "do" him: "I suppose it's flattering. I like when Chuck McCann and Dick Van Dyke do me." But, he said, there was a guy who asked to come over "and the whole time he was here he talked in my voice. It was so goddamn embarrassing I didn't know where to look."

The apartment was at best three rooms, modern furniture, with a commanding view of the sea. His honorary Oscar was on the TV, a rather small framed photo of L&H on the wall. No other showbiz mementos. We sat, with tea.

"I just today got a lovely letter. You might like to read it."

He was justly proud. It was two pages, beautifully handwritten, praising his work in films with detailed appreciations of his comic techniques, ending with, "I have always attempted to emulate you in so many ways in my work."

It was signed "Alec Guinness."

I told him how it irritated me in reading Charlie Chaplin's recent and redundantly titled *My Autobiography* that there was no mention of Laurel. And yet we learn in a photo caption that the two of them arrived on the same boat from England with the Karno troupe. I said, peevishly, "I guess the great man didn't want his historic entrance to America diluted by sharing it with another great comedian."

His sweet reply: "I don't deserve to be mentioned in the same sentence with Charlie."

Neither he nor "Babe" Hardy, as he always referred to him, got a cent of the millions raked in on their movies on TV. Stan—and he had insisted I call him that—said he didn't mind the money, but it killed him to see the films cut up to sell peanut butter and used cars.

"I hated to see the interruptions hurt the gags. I wrote to the distributor and offered to recut the films for them for free, but they never answered my letter."

"Were you never hurt? Amidst all those explosions and car wrecks and floods and crashing through floors and falling bricks and—"

"Only once. Between takes, I was talking and stepped backwards off a curb and twisted my ankle."

An eon after making their last films, Stan said the mechanism still hums. "I still dream up gags for Babe and me. The other day I thought of having a doorbell ring in the other room and Babe says, 'Stanley, go get the door.' And I come back with the door." We laughed.

Another one. Stan has had a profound thought and Ollie asks what it is. "You can't strike a match on a cake of soap." We agreed the door gag was better.

Stanley Kramer, he said, had offered him "a nice chunk of money" to appear for just a couple of quick shots in the movie *It's a Mad, Mad, Mad, Mad World*.

Stan declined. "I just didn't want the kids to see how different I look."

The phone rang and he apologized for having to deal with some business. I picked up a magazine, pretending to read, while trying to fuse the screen Laurel with the well-spoken, businesslike figure on the phone. Where in that body was the dim-witted, bleak-faced, haplessly gesturing silly we know so well?

The closest you yourself can get to this contrast is in *A Chump at Oxford*. Stan, at Oxford, is bumped hard on the head by a falling window and instantly reverts to a time in his life when he was a British lord. He plays the subsequent scenes with a faultless upper-class accent, complete with dressing gown, monocle, and long cigarette holder. He could be doing Noël Coward's *Present Laughter*. (Hilariously, he repeatedly refers to Oliver, now his manservant, as "Fatty." Ollie winces.)

He liked that I singled this out. "It's the only place people could see that maybe I'm not a total buffoon."

I asked about stories that he and Hardy never saw each other offscreen. He said rumors of feuds and coldness were phony. But there was a priceless and somewhat revealing story.

He said he dropped by Hardy's apartment with a present on Christmas morning and it was instantly clear that Hardy had gotten nothing for Stan.

"Babe sort of frantically looked around under the Christmas tree and spotted an unwrapped, very expensive bottle of bourbon. He picked it up, looked at it fondly, and apparently realized that it was *in fact* a very fine bottle of bourbon. He held it out toward me. 'You can almost never find this brand here in Los Angeles,' he said, putting it back."

Stan laughed heartily.

He told me he learned early on in directing Babe to save his "burns"—that great, full-screen, exasperated, direct-to-camera stare of Hardy's—until the end of the day, "when he couldn't wait to get out of his costume and out to the golf course before it got any later. I got some great burns that way."

Stan would stay at the studio, working into the night, editing.

A sensitive point: In my maturity, I've had to agree with Woody Allen that Hardy is the finer screen comedian. His precision of movement and delicacy of gesture are things of beauty. His work is scaled perfectly to the screen. Stan, coming from the vaudeville stage, is sometimes a bit too broad for the camera.

There is a sad quote from Hardy somewhere, wondering if he had had a valuable life, "just pulling silly faces for a camera." Oliver Hardy was an artist to his fingertips. But the affection goes to Stan.

During my visit, as he took another brief phone call, leaning back in his desk chair with his back to the sea, I noticed that the sun was beginning to set. The symbolism was a bit too much. We parted. I said good-bye, and he said, "Let's make that 'au revoir.'" What a class act.

Back at the studio I told Jack Paar where I'd been and he asked me to quickly write a brief tribute to Stan for that night's show. It played well, and Stan was delighted.

Some years later, while I was working for Johnny Carson, Stan was in the hospital for a time, and I got a letter from him that included the line, "Johnny Carson came to the hospital to visit me. Gave me quite a lift." I gave Johnny the letter; too dumb even to copy it.

Over time, more visits and letters followed right up until the time in February 1965 when I walked into Johnny's office with that day's joke submission. "You, too?" he said, dabbing his eyes. We'd both just seen the news of Stan's death come over the wires.

"Write me something, Richard," he said. I did, and with a minute to go at the end of that night's show, he did it. "A great comedian died today," it began, and a picture of Stan filled the screen. I don't remember the rest of it, but Johnny did it beautifully. His voice broke at the end.

SEPTEMBER 7, 2012

Can You Stand Some More Stan?

You overwhelmed me, dear reader, with your reaction(s) to the piece I did last time about Stan Laurel. I'm particularly moved by the number of you who were touched, using phrases like "I misted up," "I shed a tear," and even "I wept." I didn't mean to upset anyone.

I feel a little funny about admitting that, rereading the piece days later, I did at least one of the above.

At the risk of anticlimax, I can add here a few things that swam back to mind in the interval. Things I had forgotten about my golden few visits with the great man. And an event that just recurred recently.

I was in Hollywood last week working on a TV project, a pilot idea concocted by the remarkably talented John Hodgman. On my first visit with Stan, he had told me that The Steps still existed—the daunting 131 concrete steps up which he and "Babe" Hardy back-breakingly struggled and heaved the crated piano, losing it a few times, in the Oscar-winning short *The Music Box*. A classic of team comedy that bears watching at least once a year. (Get *Laurel and Hardy: The Essential Collection*.)

Several commenters on the column had a favorite moment from that film: the one when the generally sweet Stan is moved to a rare display of rage when the fuming Billy Gilbert—the intended recipient of the piano—insists they get themselves and the giant crate out of his way as he descends the stairs from his house at the top of the hill.

Stan swats his top hat off. Gilbert steams and bellows as it bounces and tumbles its way to the very bottom of the steps and rolls into the street. A truck runs over it. Stan insisted the truck move *very* slowly. It makes it funnier.

An iconic moment in film comedy.

So last week, in a break from the stuff I was shooting, as a treat for me, my dear wife arranged for a friend of ours to drive us on a pilgrimage. We found The Steps.

(The location is hardly a secret, but just for fun let's pretend I'm giving you a bit of inside information. You can find the steps yourself at the corner of Vendome and Del Monte in the Silver Lake district, just south of Sunset. There's a little grassy triangle nearby that's been named Laurel and Hardy Park. The magic numbers: 923–937 North Vendome Street.)

At first the steps look wrong, somehow, and you wonder if you've been misled. In the 1930s, they stood virtually alone; now, houses and low apartment buildings and high shrubbery surround them. Much has changed, but worshippers are rewarded by the fact that the house across the street, where the hapless boys parked their horse-drawn wagon, survives. A plaque on the bottom step reading STAN LAUREL AND OLIVER HARDY "THE MUSIC BOX" reassures you you're in the right place. I assumed it had been put there by the Laurel & Hardy–adoring organization Sons of the Desert, but in fact seems to have been placed by an impressive list of sponsors, including Hollywood Heritage Inc., the Society of Operating Cameramen, the Silent Society, the Hollywood Studio Museum, and perhaps others.

It was like visiting a holy place.

For trivialists: there are exactly 131 steps. We climbed them as an act of homage.

Don't be disappointed to learn that there is in fact no house of Billy Gilbert's at the top. There never was. It was a studio set.

Another bit of arcana. The same steps were used by the boys for a 1927 film called *Hats Off!* Alas, the search for this lost gem goes on.

Stan recalled a favorite moment in *The Music Box*: "Remember the baby nurse lady who's pushing the baby carriage who laughs at us? And how when she turns her back, I kick her in the butt? And she tells a cop and he says, 'He kicked you?' I asked for another take and added a line for her that might have been thought vaguely naughty, but I knew the kids wouldn't get it but the sharper adults would. I had her say: 'Yes, officer. He kicked me. Right in the middle of my daily duties.'"

We laughed.

How I could have temporarily forgotten a certain revelation by Stan I can't imagine. He talked about the time when he and Hardy were suddenly surprised by the oleaginous Ralph Edwards and lured, live, on the spot, onto his *This Is Your Life* TV show. Rudely surprised by Edwards's crew and suddenly flooded with light while peacefully chatting with their wives and a friend in a hotel lounge, they were to be spirited quickly to Edwards's studio a few blocks away for the live show, but Hardy rebelled.

Stan: "Babe was livid. He was halfway into his car to go straight home, leaving poor Ralph sweating in the studio with half a guest list. Babe reluctantly relented."

It's their only live television appearance and should have been wonderful. It's around, but it is infuriating to watch. The endlessly yakking Edwards—phony as his hairpiece—does all the talking. He raises a subject and, instead of saying to the pair, "Tell us about that"—*he* tells us.

You wish Stan would treat him like Billy Gilbert and swat his rug off.

You long to hear them talk. Edwards allows them each a few words while repeatedly attempting witless jokes about the life-threateningly obese Hardy's girth. Babe plays along with faux pleasantry as surprise guests like Hal Roach, their former employer, and a few relatives are awkwardly trotted out. Eventually and mercifully the travesty ends.

It should be avoided as ardently as—and I apologize for this dirty word—the "colorized" version of *The Music Box*, which is still floating around. Miraculously, the cheesy colorizing practice—now junked—manages to extract all humor from the great film. A subject for an essay on the inferiority of color to black-and-white. (Sorry, young folks who boast of watching no movies not multihued. There really are a few good black-and-white ones.)

This is interesting: One reader pointed out the coincidence that when my first column ran, the BBC radio was airing a show about L&H. I listened to it online. Somehow I joined it in the middle and a man was talking. The voice was not familiar. He was talking about how Babe Hardy took no responsibility for the films, had no interest in the editing, and wanted out as early as possible so he could escape to the golf course. And how he, the speaker, worked far into the night. It had to be a stranger reading a quote from Stan Laurel. But it was Stan Laurel.

Here again is something I'd forgotten. Stan's real voice, in conversation, was not the voice of "Stan" in the movies. It was about ten notes lower. While not falsetto, his character voice used in the films was at least an octave higher than his own. His real voice was nearer baritone. I've never seen this mentioned.

I'll close with a little gem from my all-too-skimpy, semi-legible and fading notes of my first meeting with Stan. We talked about what he liked and didn't like on television. "There's one television show, lad"—I was twenty-four!—"that I just can't abide. It's the one with that panel of ultra-chichi folks. The one called *What's My Line?* It sends me straight up the wall. I call it *The Snob Family.*"

A man for the ages.

OCTOBER 5, 2012

How Are the Mighty Fallen, or Where's My Friend?

D o you have things you mean to do, and ought to do, but don't? What is that? People you suspect are saner than yourself simply say: "Just go ahead and *do* it. What's stopping you?" You agree. It's sensible and should be done. But you don't do it and you sit there and it starts to slip from your mind and you pick up an unread *Vanity Fair* or *The Farmer's Almanac* and another year goes by.

That's how it was with me and Muhammad Ali. I mean, with Muhammad Ali and me.

This will sound funny—peculiar to some—but there was a period in my life when I felt that Muhammad Ali was my best friend.

I don't mean an imaginary, worshipped from afar friend but a worshipped from "anear" one. He was on my shows a whole lot of times, we saw each other offstage and on, and the champ appeared to have a real fondness for me. I, of course, loved that and developed a deep affection for him.

Years went by, his world and mine diverged, and about the time I realized we hadn't horsed around together—neither offstage nor on—in quite a while, his illness struck.

The thing put off was about my desire to see him again when he became ill, along with, I hope, an understandable reluctance to see that great eminence reduced by sickness. Years went by. And more years, and he got worse. I'll never get over the regret. What was my psychoanalysis good for if I didn't go and see my ailing friend?

Finally, if not inevitably, circumstances brought us together again.

The Norman Mailer Center gives awards to writers, and this, some weeks back, was its annual banquet. Ali and Mailer were friends, and Ali was the gala's guest of honor. Among the distinguished guest speakers were such folks as Oliver Stone, Joyce Carol Oates (a boxing fan), Garrison Keillor, the LBJ immortalizer Robert Caro, and, deftly and wittily emceeing, Alec Baldwin.

Events like this are always a seemingly unavoidable combination of sleep-inducing ennui and excessive length and make me swear if I ever get home from this one and to bed, I'll never go to another one or to anything else. Ever.

This was the exception. Ingeniously staged by the movie producer, writer, etc. Lawrence Schiller in the Mandarin Oriental Hotel's imperial ballroom in Manhattan, this was a model of how to do it. With one especially tough problem to crack: how to present the largely immobilized guest of honor.

Schiller's solution: there was the usual center-of-attention stage with mike and lectern, but also a second one. In another part of the room a small theater was constructed with a well-raised stage and a handsome, closed curtain.

The champ had quietly been placed there, and when he was introduced and the curtain revealed him, the elegant crowd, at their elegant tables, went mad.

There, seated on what amounted to a throne, tuxedoed and in wraparound dark, dark glasses, sat the arguably greatest athlete of all time. The applause rolled on. He looked like an African emperor out of some romantic tale.

A few of us, including his heroic wife, Lonnie, spoke briefly and reminisced, and the curtains closed. With much help, he was brought to a nearby table.

Before dinner, for a sizable fee, for a good cause, of course, you could sit on a couch beside him and have your picture taken with the only three-time heavyweight champion of the world. A long line of well-heeled folk did before returning to, at the top of the scale, their $100,000 tables.

Ali sat looking straight ahead and didn't speak. While waiting for the line to clear, I asked Lonnie if there was any chance he'd remember me. She said there was a good chance, "but the problem is he can't speak to you. He can't answer you."

I sat beside him and began a one-sided chat. It was a bit like talking to a statue, his features drawn downward by the illness and seemingly frozen. I'm not sure I would have recognized him.

I kept talking in hopes of some sign, and after I'd said my name a few times and recalled fun and funny incidents from our good times together, the frozen-looking countenance continued to stare straight ahead. But then it stirred a little, and I hoped desperately he might turn toward me, or at least mouth my name—my mixed-blessingly recognizable voice seemed suddenly to have gotten through. It was not to be. But I honestly think—or maybe I just need to think—that a bell rang.

Suddenly a large woman hove into view and said snippily, "We have a lot of people waiting in line." I was being bounced. In fact, there were but three people waiting, and they were enjoying watching the two of us and were not irked.

I wasted a good and useful line from *Measure for Measure* on her.

" 'Dress'd in a little brief authority,' are we?" I asked. After a bit longer, I moved away. There wasn't much more to do or say.

Boxing.

It's a brutish and disgusting sport and should probably be outlawed. (Sorry, Norman.)

Few doubt that Ali's sad state was caused by head blows, akin to NFL cranium smashing. At the same time, paradoxically, it's an entertaining sport and, at its best, requires and demonstrates great skills, complex strategies, and mastery of technique.

That's what sets it apart—way apart—from that moron's Punch and Judy show laughingly called "professional wrestling." That sleazy, painstakingly rehearsed game of charades that requires more thespian skill than athletic prowess. A "manly art" requiring about as much manliness as crocheting.

Paradoxically, what many describe as "men battering each other senseless" approaches, at its highest level, art. Should you need convincing on this, get ahold of the great A. J. Liebling's masterpiece on the subject, *The Sweet Science*.

This is a silly sort of speculation, but would anyone suggest that given the magical choice of reliving his life Parkinson's-free, Ali would gladly make the trade-off? Forsaking all those years of glory as the Most Famous Person in the World?

In that notorious survey, the Ali face proved to be the only one among the world's most famous visages past and present instantly recognized in even the remotest parts of the planet. No other face was. Not Elvis, not JFK, not Mickey Mouse, not Jackie, not Honest Abe, Mick, or Marilyn. In the most far-flung regions, there was only one face pointed to by the Bantu tribesman and a farmer's wife in rural Tibet. Pointed to with "Ali, Ali."

Had you come from way down, as young Cassius Clay did, would you trade all that? For health? I don't suggest that the answer is an obvious one.

At this point, a self-imposed word count prevents me from detailing some of the ways the Champ and I had offstage fun together. Another time?

OCTOBER 26, 2012

Ali, Round Two

One day, the champ asked if I'd like to see his training camp—he was preparing for his 1974 fight with Joe Frazier—and someone suggested taking cameras and making a show out of it. Whoever that was was smart.

The camp was unique, situated in a delightful rural setting in Pennsylvania. Great effort had gone into making the place primitive, as Ali says, twice, "like in the days of Jack Johnson."

He delighted in showing me his private cabin, and in using the words "antique" and the tautology "old antique" to describe the furnishings. He was like a big, exuberant kid, showing off his hideout. He was—and there's no other word—sweet. And it was also, of course, a skillful performance by a master.

There was a bit of acting on my part, too, as in pretending in his gym, for alleged comic purposes, that I couldn't jump rope.

(And I can't conceive of why I said to him that I wrestled in high school when one could plainly see from my bared body that I was a gymnast.)

I was put into a bedroom with the décor of a western lodge. No sign of Ali. Suddenly the door exploded open and a rowdy gang of my host and a group of his buddies burst into the room and flopped and draped themselves on the ample bed. They were a lively bunch, carousing like high school or fraternity pals: mock insults, playful punching, and general horsing around, all the elements of adolescent boy fun with plenty of laughter.

Ali kept announcing, with an artful-seeming seriousness, "I

can't believe Dick Cavett came all the way to Pennsylvania just to see me!" Oddly, I can't recall for sure if I stayed overnight. He did once at my place, but that's a separate story.

His mother somehow cooked and served a hearty lunch for about twenty: TV crew, hangers-on, the jostling buddies, assorted relatives.

Halfway through lunch I noticed a certain conspiring and giggling among Ali and his buddies and then, lowering his voice so his mom wouldn't hear, he whispered, "We got some company for you, Dick. Look what just came in." I turned toward the door to see two of the most pleasant-seeming and startlingly unattractive women ever created. Had the pranksters used Central Casting?

Ali: "No hurry, Dick. They can stay all night."

Delight at my discomfort filled the room. One of the buddies nearly choked to death on a combination of my consternation, his laughter, and a half-swallowed chunk of soul food. The merry jest over, the ladies were whisked away, in transportation that had been neatly arranged, and they were, I learned, generously rewarded.

I never figured out how to get even. Maybe that's why I used the word *niggardly* to him on a show, rewarded by the famous hands closing about my neck as he pretended not to know what it meant.

I promised last time to report some of the odd, fun, goofy sort of things that would happen between us. What follows won't sound, at first, like fun, but it gets there.

We were both part of some documentary back in those wonderful healthy days, and when I arrived on the "set" (a dune by the sea in Montauk), although the weather was fine, there was thick gloom. Muhammad was in a funk. I'd heard about these.

The filmmakers were looking desperate. "He won't talk to anybody and he just stands there gazing out to sea. We can't get to him. It's like he doesn't hear you." They were about to pack it in. They asked me to try to do something.

The champ stood there staring out to sea, statue-motionless, looking like an extraordinarily handsome cigar-store Indian. (I refuse to say "cigar-store Native American.")

I approached warily.

"Ali?" I ventured. He turned. And he burst into glee. "Dick Cavett!" he shouted, arms around me. Had he forgotten I was in it?

All was fine now, and the director, virtually in tears of gratitude, seemed to shed ten years.

"What's this effect you have on him?" he wondered.

I can't begin to explain it. What was I to him who, then, had everything? What was our curious bond?

Opinions solicited.

At the end of the documentary shooting in Montauk, it was getting dark and I volunteered to drive the Champ to his motel where his (then) wife, the beautiful Veronica, was waiting, and we all had dinner.

I like watching people's behavior when they recognize the famous, but with Ali it was unique.

He saw me to my car in front of the motel. Sometimes I would sort of forget who it was I was with until, as in this case, a couple going for their car saw him standing by mine and lost the power of speech.

The woman could only unconsciously keep pointing while her dumbstruck husband, trying to exclaim, only managed to phonate a sort of protracted "oooorg" sound, his eyes having dilated to a larger size. I guess it was as Woody Allen said when he first laid eyes, at his new job, on Sid Caesar: "It was like looking at a god."

Later, as I started the car, Ali suddenly said, "Hey, Dick, how far's your house? I wanna see it." He jumped in. (No mention of Veronica.) It was only five minutes away.

He loved the place and I said, "You don't want to stay in a motel tonight, man. Why don't you stay here?"

"Hey, Dick, you really mean that? My friends won't ever believe I stayed in Dick Cavett's house." As I was about to match him with what *my* friends wouldn't believe, he added, "My mama really won't believe it."

"She wouldn't accusing you of fibbing, call you 'Cassius,' and, as they say down in Dixie, 'slap you upside the head'?" (*Big laugh.*)

"Hey, Dick, you not only sound like my mama, you starting to look like her." (*My turn to convulse.*)

He asked if there was a bed for him and his wife. Of course, the master bedroom bed was offered and he got into it. "Will you go get Veronica while I lie down?" I did. He switched on the TV.

When we got back he was giggling to himself over what had just happened.

My late wife, Carrie Nye, was then in a play in New York. The phone had rung and Ali had picked it up.

My answering machine recorded this much of the conversation:

(*Ringing.*)
Ali: Hello.
C.N.: Darling?
Ali: This ain't Darling.
C.N.: I'm sorry, I—Who is this?
Ali: Who is this? It's the only three-time heavyweight champion of the world and I'm sleepin' in your bed and I'm watchin' your TV.
C.N. (*after a moment*): Well, Mr. Ali, I shall have a plaque placed on that bed.
(*An offer she never made me.*)

The answering machine cut out there. Glad I had a wife who knew what—and especially who—the "heavyweight champion" was. How things have changed. How many wives today could name the heavyweight champion? And how many husbands? I can't.

I told this story on television and one night after that, at about 2 a.m., my phone rang. A gravelly, menacing, unfamiliar voice said, "Hey, Dick Cavett. I hear you lettin' niggers sleep in your bed."

While I was trying to think what a book on anger management might advise as to the best thing to do or say here, there was an ominous silence. Then a kind of chilling gurgling sound. Then the Voice of the Anonymous Coward let out a laugh that was both hearty and, now, somehow familiar.

Perhaps you can guess who it was?

Writing this stuff continues to dredge up memories and subjects about this great man. I sometimes think I may have enough good stuff to write about him until the next Romney administration.

Looking at him in the old clips, he is in the midst of the best part of his life. Being with him, I felt that I was, too.

NOVEMBER 16, 2012

Back When I Was Packing

I know what it feels like to be a gun lover.

As a kid watching Saturday afternoon World War II movies in Nebraska, I fell head over heels in love. With the Luger. I don't expect more than a handful of folks to know what I'm talking about. But it was real and it was intense; terms usually associated, I know, with a love affair. The human sort.

There is something about a Luger that separates it from all other handguns, and Luger devotees and Luger society members speak of it in romantic terms that must sound plain nuts to those who consider themselves levelheaded.

I sat in the dark and watched Helmut Dantine, the downed German flier in *Mrs. Miniver*, menace Greer Garson with his Luger and, yes, I dreamed that night that he came to Grand Island, Nebraska, and gave the gun to me.

No other gun has ever appealed to me in the least.

Charles "Peanuts" Schulz said on my show that he "brought home a bag of 'em" from the war. Seeing me nearly swoon with envy, he added, "I'll send you one."

I gasped. I wish he had.

Time went by, about a decade's worth, and I accompanied a friend to a gun show in Los Angeles.

And I bought a Luger. Easy. No questions asked. Like buying a candy bar. My friend was a friend of a dealer. I signed nothing other than a check.

If you prefer not to think me a loon, you might want to skip the next part.

I took my treasure back to my hotel and spent an hour or more in front of a full-length mirror being, alternately, Conrad Veidt, Ivan Triesault, Eduardo Ciannelli, Walter Slezak, and probably ten other of those splendid European actors who always seemed to be playing Nazi officers in the war movies of the 1940s and '50s.

And you might as well know the worst: I slept with it.

I think the degree to which this resembles a sexual confession is not entirely coincidental. Learnèd (two-syllable pronunciation) papers and studies exist on the sexuality of guns, focusing always on the rather obvious phallic resemblance of the handheld gun and the male organ; comfortable grip, extension, ejection, consequences of improper use . . . the list goes on.

The gun-confiscation paranoid mind-set is seen in these studies as—what else?—castration fear. And there's the unfailing potency of the gun as a substitute for the failing potency of, well, you know. As Gore Vidal said, you can always get your gun up.

Because I couldn't take my prize possession to New York, I left it with my friend in L.A. He died, and I never saw it again. (I make do with a frighteningly perfect scale model.)

Hasn't just about everything possible been said about the death of the children at Sandy Hook Elementary School? And the gun laws that have made this country the sick joke of the world?

And, as always, there were some things that shouldn't have been said.

The raving speech by the NRA's boy, Wayne La Pierre, for example, urging more guns in schools as the answer.

I had Wayne as a guest on the show once. He may not remember, because I'm not sure he ever saw me. His eyes and consciousness seem to bypass you somehow, and focus somewhere in an undefined middle distance. The words sound memorized; he has an affect that might best be described as "nobody home."

Maybe you saw Bob Costas—before the roof caved in on him—make the reasonable observation, after the football player Jovan Belcher shot his girlfriend and then himself, that had he not had a gun, they might be alive. Many were outraged by Costas. You'd have thought he had painted obscenities on the Statue of Liberty. How dare a sportscaster sully the sacred atmosphere of a sports event with a thought?

Costas was berated on Don Imus's show by the usually intelligent Laura Ingraham with one of those why-blame-the-gun mental quirks so compatible with the right-wing mind. (Her segment was wickedly utilized by Jon Stewart.)

As her version of "Guns don't kill people . . . ," she wondered whether Costas thought the football player wasn't strong enough to *strangle* the woman? Well, for one thing, there are survivable attempted stranglings. Significantly fewer folks survive close-range gun blasts. But let's say that being gunless, he *does* manage manually to throttle the girl. Then what? He goes to that parking lot and, in front of two observers, strangles *himself*?

One of the worst things said in the awful succeeding days—though it wasn't nearly at Mike Huckabee–level inanity—came, surprisingly, straight from the White House. I was appalled to see the president ruin a movingly delivered statement about the shooting of the kids by closing with "God has called them all home."

Talk about not blaming the shooter. So it was God who did it. It's not hard to imagine a kid hearing the president's words and asking, "Mommy, is God going to call me home?"

One of the main tenets of the true gun-crazies—and the N.R.A. is not even the most rabid of the many gun-shielding organizations—is, as Rachel Maddow expertly delineated, that old standby "the first step."

There are online forms you can fill out to send to your lawmakers, demanding that nothing—nothing at all or in any way—be done about any guns whatever, anywhere. Not assault rifles, not the super-magazines that allowed the kids to be ripped apart, nothing.

Why?

Because it is the *first step* toward confiscation.

The mind falls faint. Nobody is going to try to confiscate guns, although some Web sites know better: President Obama, they are certain, wants to.

And, of course, all first steps are but first steps. Thus, all kisses lead to pregnancy, a single joint leads to heroin, a Band-Aid leads to surgery. Can't I take a first step toward China without going to China? Oh, well.

Reading this over, I'm not really sure what the first part about me and my Luger has to do with all this. Perhaps qualified people among you will tell me.

I'm not going to worry about it. After all, for me, it might just be a *first step* toward self-criticism.

JANUARY 11, 2013

More on Guns, with Readers

It's happened again. I'm impressed by my readers.

Is this base flattery?

In spite of our ailing educational system, which allows our students to rank in discouraging positions like thirteenth, twenty-fourth, thirty-seventh, or whatever against the world in little things like math, science, engineering, etc., I keep seeing, right here, evidence that lots and lots of people have not dumbed down.

Or if they have, they must have been spectacularly smart and literate before.

I base this on the fact of so many splendid, thoughtful e-mails in response to this (and other) columns and articles. There's nothing I want to do less than write on the subject of guns again. But the fact that "Back When I Was Packing" drew such a large number and sterling quality of e-mails changed my mind. I decided that a nice person wouldn't ignore so many concerned readers.

Why do you suppose so many people in supposedly postliterate America—despite how many of our language and brain skills have been rubbed dull by overexposure to computer games and reality shows and iPods and John McCain running mates—can still just plain write well.

Here's an example of clean writing that teachers wish they could easily teach; from Terry of Nevada.

> I find the confiscatory argument strange. It's usually put
> forward by folks who fear that their government will

take their rights away and, lacking guns, they will have no defense against that.

Oddly these same people often advocate for a strong military. Do these people seriously believe that some sort of people's militia will be any match for the military they've helped to create, if the military were under the control of some despot? A few guys standing around with Bushmasters are going to defeat, say, the guys who took out bin Laden?

Yes, Terry, it would take extremely skillful Bushmaster wielders to hold out for long against that same evil government's jet bombers, rocket grenades, tear gas, offshore gunships, heavy-duty cannons, and napalm. Not to mention drones.

And, of course, its well-trained militia.

We're told that succeeding in making those military-style super guns with their massacre-a-whole-crowd magazines no longer readily available to our lunatics, or at least the lunatics who don't already own them, is an admirable goal.

But apparently it would be but a minor step, owing to the fact that the more lowly handgun is still the real villain, far and away the weapon of choice in our countless killings. We're told those he-man big-boy guns account for but 1 percent of our scandalous death rate. And not even all of our mass killers used them.

The thought hit me, after the longest time, that all the mass shooters have been men. Some will ask why that should surprise anyone.

I e-mailed the thought to Don Imus on the air and he asked his guests, two women, if they'd heard or read of female mass killers. They reached back and came up with the woman who drowned all her kids, and then farther back to Fall River's famous citizen and skilled rap beater, Lizzie Borden. They're women, for sure, and their murders were at least kept in the family, but they weren't multiple shooters.

There have been, of course, numerous one-offs by women, mainly against erring husbands and lovers.

Ah, but we spoke too soon. Don't miss the February 11, 2013, issue of *The New Yorker* for the chilling exception ("A Loaded Gun," by Patrick Radden Keefe).

Someone pointed out that the NRA has more than one thing in mind when it diabolically proposes an armed guard in every school. As is well known, the organization—still humorously claiming to be about gun safety—and gun manufacturers are joined at the waist as securely as Chang and Eng, the famous Siamese twins. If only one hundred thousand schools subscribed to the plan, that would be . . . let's see now . . . how many gun sales?

Here's a grim little parlor game. Ask someone how many United States shootings they think there have been since Newtown. I got answers ranging from not having heard of any to guessing probably a dozen or so.

Wanna play? Before you make a bet, here is but a handful of Googlables that might help.

"Over 1600 Hundred Gun-Related Deaths Since Newtown"

"3 School Shootings Since Newtown"

"Shootings killed 18 people in US per day since Sandy Hook, study shows"

So what is the melancholy conclusion to be drawn from all this?

Doesn't it appear that the best thing you and I, as Americans, can do as protection against getting shot at any moment is to, without delay, move to any other country on the planet? So it would seem.

Is it too dramatic to ask what rough beast is gnawing at the soul of America?

Let us close with something in a lighter vein.

When I was a kid in Nebraska, a cantankerous farmer, known for plinking with his .22 at passing cars in which he perceived enemies, ingeniously rigged up a shotgun in his house, trained on the inside of his front door so as to widely distribute any intruder.

It seems he was a touch forgetful . . .

I'm sure my brighter students can finish this story.

FEBRUARY 8, 2013

And the Oscar Doesn't Go to the Oscars

Well, here we are again. Oscar has come and gone.

Words to gladden the heart. E'en so, fair warning. This *will* be about Oscar. I won't be hurt if you decide to read something else.

My problem with Oscar always begins with the first utterance of those dread words, "I'd like to thank . . ." My hands involuntarily reach for the Bayer bottle and a Tum.

When they come to their senses and make me commissar of the Oscar show, I promise you this: anyone uttering those brain-numbing words and attempting to thank more than three people will be instantly dropped through a trapdoor.

It will be well padded down below. No one wants anyone to get hurt.

There'll be coffee down there, and magazines. But there will be no egress from the nice and comfortable subterranean chamber until the show has faded from the screen. No reclaiming the stage, clutching what looks like a toilet paper roll of thank-you's.

Why was this fungus allowed to creep all over what used to be a lot of fun to watch?

Get ready to Google or iPad or whatever, young folks, but there was a time before Oscar became the Festival of Thanks, when a man who went by the name Bob Hope delivered such gems as, "Well, here we are again at Oscar Night. Or as it's known at my house, Passover."

I'm not sure I've recovered fully from the night the divine

Julia Roberts thanked all but four people in the Los Angeles phone book. They got halfway through Beethoven's Fifth trying to play her off.

The same question arises about Oscar that I ask myself every year about the Bowl that is allegedly Super. Why do I watch it? (Okay, this year's game *was* good.)

I really need to know why we inflict such punishment on ourselves.

Can I say nothing nice about old Osky? I can. They do, in one area at least, seem to have given me less and less reason to mutter aloud, "Will they never learn?" I'm talking about those dreadful, invariably bombing two-person "comedy" bits that, over the years, they've saddled the presenters with. They are blessedly fewer, but still.

You know the ones I mean.

Tom: Hi, Jan. Say, that's some dress you're wearing. (*Delivered while staring straight out front by a guy who seems to be wearing a tux for the first time. And welded to the prompter, which always seems to be a yard too far away. The dialogue is of pure wood.*)

Jan: Oh, thanks, Tom. I'm so glad you care for my dress, as I made it myself at my home.

Tom: Wow. (*Delivered without emphasis or energy.*) Well, I sure hope you make it home still in it. (*Strangled mercy laugh.*)

I'm sorry. My made-up example is far too funny to be typical of the genre, but you know what I mean.

And I'm sorry to say that some very good actors, when dipping a first-time toe into comedy, need to be given, as foreign actors do, "line readings." In order, that is, to prevent the "That was no lady, that was MY wife" problem.

How old an oldie must you be to remember that there was a time before innocent awards viewers, just looking for a little fun, were subjected to these paralyzing paroxysms of imaginary gratitude?

Imaginary, I say, because what is it all really saying?

It's saying, "I really don't deserve this award. No, no. It's not for me at all. Not at all. It really belongs to a *lot* of people . . ."

Like hell. You gave the performance, they didn't. The false modesty is thick and of high viscosity.

Here's the kind of thing you endure. Effusions of thanks and salivating affection for such household names as:

Henny Goldfarb. And Janey Dillman . . . and Clyde Whale . . . and Sneed Hearn . . . and Tomm, my best buddy . . . and the incredible Eldridge Endrubber . . . and, of course, Alvira Winkle . . . and dear, dear Conchita for, well, just about everything . . . and the girls in the Huppman office, and darling "Chummy" . . . you know who you are. Oh, and André, my masseur [*oddly, pronounced "massooss"*] . . . oh, and at the Morris Agency, Schmul Yamazaki . . . and Cheech Bolander, my neighbor who never fails to, like, water my plants, oh, and Floyd for, well, just for being Floyd . . . and for undying affection when I need it most, dearest Pootie and Tootie, my two Shih Tzus . . . and of course a very special Mom . . . and Dearest Dad, who I know is looking down on us right now [*from where, up in the flies?*] and, oh, don't play me off, I've got one more list somewhere here. Ah, yes, and . . . [*a shot rings out*] . . .

A fantasy? An exaggeration? Just ask yourself.

A radical idea I know, but couldn't Sneed and Eldridge and that whole lot be thanked off-camera, with a nice note and maybe a modest gift or two? A caringly wrapped case of Tootsie Rolls and some nice hollyhocks?

Here is a typical Oscar thank-you from the good old days, an artifact from a far-off, happier time before it occurred to anyone to bore us to idiocy with a list of unheard-of strangers. Somewhere on the Net I found an acceptance speech by the great David Niven. It went:

"And the winner is . . . *David Niven!*" (*Affectionate ovation.*)

Niven: "Thank you. I'm so weighed down with good luck amulets and charms from friends that I was barely able to struggle my way up here onto the stage. I'm very grateful." (Exits.)

Where are the Nivens of yesteryear?

A shame, in a way, that he didn't say more, because I recall Niven as a scintillating guest on an early show of mine. His talk simply sparkled and was compared favorably—presumably by some rather elderly people—to that of Oscar Wilde.

Nobody that year read a gratitude laundry list. Though a helpful friend reminds me that Greer Garson, in 1943, established the all-time record for speech length. When she got home, two of her children had grown up during it.

I confess I still retain some affection for Oscar. I know the reviews weren't very good this year and I know it's easy to kick Oscar when he's down.

But then when is he up?

MARCH 1, 2013

Tonight, Tonight, Its World Is Full of Blight

Once again, *The Tonight Show* rears its hoary head in the headlines. (Unintentional wordplay.)

The dear old thing, the brainchild of the great Pat Weaver (Sigourney's pop), has endured as if it were a World War II veteran surviving health crisis after health crisis over the years, defying demise.

For me, addicted watching began with Jack Paar. When Jack departed the show for good in 1962—having left it temporarily once already—it was predicted that *Tonight* would die on the vine. Who could replace that sentimental, explosive, compellingly neurotic master of late-night? And where would you even begin to look for such a one?

The answer came. The boyishly nice-looking guy from Nebraska, collegiate and witty, who killed 'em out of the public eye at Friars roasts and trade lunches while hosting the ungrammatically named game show *Who Do You Trust?* (TV's earliest dumbing down?)

The powers could breathe easily. The *Tonight* cash cow, without Jack, would not one day be found dead in the pasture.

And now, for a little-remembered fact: It didn't go well for Johnny Carson at first. Hard to believe in light of his smashing thirty-year endurance record at that desk.

Let me take you back. A now forgotten summer passed between Jack's exit and Johnny's debut. There were contract matters, but Johnny also well knew it would have been unwise, with Jack's departing good-bye wave still fresh in bereft viewers' minds, to pop brightly onto his predecessor's stage as the clean-cut but resented new boy.

And there was another factor. It was called Merv Griffin.

A virtual mob of substitute hosts that summer—and oh, did I write for them—included not only Merv but various comics, movie stars, Groucho Marx, Mort Sahl, Art Linkletter (let's keep moving), Donald O'Connor (!), Jerry Lewis, a Gabor, and on and on, all trying their variously talented hands at what Jack made look easy.

Merv did two weeks sensationally. Johnny spent a goodly amount of awkward between-jobs time that summer in his high-rise apartment over the East River with his drums, his telescope, and his compulsive reading, practicing his card sleights and then having to endure a gradually rising tide of articles and column items about how Merv had clearly demonstrated that *he* should have been the one to get *The Tonight Show*.

I could never figure out why there seemed to be an almost organized campaign to take the show back from Johnny before he ever got it. Merv, not above, shall we say, dedicated self-interest, was to my mind probably quietly instrumental in much of this. But then who, in our business, never known for being full of selfless sweethearts, would not fight at least tooth, if not nail, for the Big Prize?

If you were around then and aware, I'll bet you've suppressed, repressed, or forgotten that Merv, while not getting *the* show, did get his own duplicate of *Tonight* on NBC daytime. The two shows made their debuts at the same time. Merv got the good reviews.

(Being a brash lad, I summoned the testicularity at the time to ask Johnny his thoughts on Merv as chat show host. Came the reply, "A case of the bland leading the bland.")

In the words of the TV scribes, Johnny was "stiff," "awkward," "uncomfortable," and even "phony." Merv, on the contrary, was hailed with a list of "up" adjectives: "bright," "clever," "sharp," "sincere," and "a good listener."

I insert a name-drop here: I was startled to hear the astute "Fat Jack" Leonard say, backstage at a benefit, "I'm sorry, but that Carson guy ain't makin' it."

He wasn't all wrong. Johnny took a slow slide into the job before hitting his stride. At first it was painful to watch, and agony for him. Who would believe this now, familiar with only his later years?

Pundits agreed, NBC had made a mistake.

Hard as the fact is to digest in light of Johnny's decades on that throne, insiders assured us it was, as one columnist put it, just a matter of time for Mr. Carson.

And of course, how right that was.

It was a mere three decades.

I've been asked for comments by various columnists and publications these days, what with the *T. Show* back in the news with the Leno-Fallon-Kimmel eruption. NBC must have a bushel-sized bottle of Bayer product in their infirmary labeled "Recurrent *Tonight Show* Headaches." There's probably enough material for a series in the various *Tonight* traumas over the years, with episodes titled, "Jack Walks"; "Jack Returns"; "Johnny Arrives"; "Johnny Struggles, Then Triumphs"; "Jay Soars"; "Jay Demoted"; "Conan at Bat"; "Bye-Bye, Conan"; "Jay Redux"; "Kimmel Threatens"; "Fallon on the Rise"; "Jay Re-Threatened"; and so on, into the late night.

Ironically, all this takes place at a time when there are articles, including one in 2010 in *The New Yorker*, about how late-night talk is doomed to be a fading commodity.

I've been widely asked about the reported building of a new set for our East Coast Jimmy—whether I'm among those who think *Tonight* belongs in Manhattan. Yes. And it always did.

James Barron quoted me in *The New York Times* as saying that for me the show was always "a lifeline to New York." When home in Nebraska on visits during college, it was my fix.

(I, too, shared the lifeline honor. More than once I'd hear from a touring actor tired of the exhausting town-to-town trouping: *After our show, on the road, we'd go back to the hotel room in Detroit or Omaha or Klamath Falls, pour a drink, and say, "Switch on Cavett, quick, for some New York oxygen."*)

Jack started it and all of us took our shows to L.A. from time to time for a fortnight. I can't say why, exactly, but *Tonight* just means Gotham, in the same way that Grand Central would just look wrong in Burbank.

Bit of a scoop? Once when I was on with Johnny out there after his coast move, in a moment of confidential frankness during a commercial, he whispered, "Richard, I'm not convinced yet that this was one of my genius ideas."

Another time, when I was a guest with Johnny not long after he'd started his cut-down-to-an-hour shows, he told me backstage that he'd convinced himself that the cutting back would seem easier and shorter. And that, to his surprise, it didn't. And sadly, he was happiest, by far, when "on."

When growing up out there in the West, both Johnny and I (at separate times) dreamed the traditional dream of the bright lights of Broadway and the glamour of Manhattan. New York, New York was our craved Shangri-la. Not the La Brea Tar Pits.

If my friend Dave Letterman should decide next contract time that he's sat through one too many starlet guests who come on to plug their movies, exhibit seemingly a yard of bare gam, pepper their speech with "like" and "I'm like" and "awesome" and "oh, wow" and "amazing," and list at least seven things they are "excited" about despite the evidence, from who knows what cause, of their half-mast eyelids, I'll regret his going.

And speaking of Dave's presumably stepping aside some sad day, if CBS is smart, there is in full view a self-evident successor to the Big L. of Indiana.

The man I'm thinking of has pulled off a miraculous, sustained feat, against all predictions—descendants of those same wise heads who foresaw a truncated run for the Carson boy—of making a smashing success while conducting his show for years with a dual personality. And I don't mean Rush Limbaugh (success without personality).

I can testify, as can anyone who's met him and seen him as himself, how much more there is to Stephen Colbert than the genius job he does in his "role" on *The Colbert Report*. Everything about him—as himself—qualifies him for that chair at the Ed Sullivan Theater that Letterman has so deftly and expertly warmed for so long. Colbert is, among other virtues, endowed with a first-rate mind, a great ad-lib wit, skilled comic movement and gesture, fine education, seemingly unlimited knowledge of affairs and events, and, from delightful occasional evidence, those things called the Liberal Arts—I'll bet you he could name the author of *Peregrine Pickle*. And on top of that largesse of qualities (and I hope he won't take me the wrong way here), good looks.

Should such a day come, don't blow it, CBS.

MARCH 29, 2013

With Winters Gone, Can We Be Far Behind?

No more Jonathan Winters.

What did we do to deserve this?

I'm just antique enough to remember when Jonathan first hit. Or at least for me. It was the Jack Paar *Tonight Show* and no one had ever seen anything remotely like it.

A slightly chubby, amiable, Midwesternly looking man who could have been an accountant or a bus driver, nicely dressed in dark suit and tie, stepped out, a bit timorously, from behind the curtain and, on the spot and before our eyes, created a whole mad little world.

There were sudden, instant changes of character, gender, and manner, each with a new face, a different voice, even different physique, it seemed.

Make that *lightning* character changes, switching in less than an eye wink from an old person to a juvenile, from tough drill sergeant to mincing hairdresser, from adult human to feisty feline, from bumpkin to society type to rube to sophisticate; from iron-jawed right-winger to gelatinous liberal, from adult to child to repellently cute baby; each change so fast and total it was as if frames had been cut from a film.

Here was originality personified. And unprecedented.

Never had a comic done anything remotely like this. Jonathan was born full-blown from the head of no one. He was in no known comic tradition. No familiar style. No pre-existing category of humor. He stood on no predecessors' shoulders.

Here, suddenly, was a comedian who never told a joke.

Into the world of humor a new planet had been born.

Later, when working for Paar, I loved watching Jonathan backstage at the show, near airtime and still trying to decide what he was going to come on as that night: A drunken kitty cat? The queen of the Vikings? A doorknob?

One night, probing in the costume room, he had found a sort of wraparound turban-shaped piece of headgear, helmet-sized and seemingly made of dark, fresh earth with twigs and sprigs of little plants protruding. Jack didn't know what was about to hit him.

Jonathan daintily flounced into the chair beside an astonished Jack and announced, giggling and crinkling up his eyes, "I'm the Spirit of Spring!"

The hat thing had two little horns, which he'd tweak now and then, with seductive winks at Jack.

Because of the character's, shall we say, lack of testosterone, there was the following exchange:

Jack: "What *are* you, anyway?"
Jonathan (sweetly): "They know in the forest."

The line killed.

A troop of *Tonight* employees would repair, after the show, with Jonathan and his *Tonight* staffer friends John Carsey and Bob Shanks and Tom O'Malley and other imbibing buddies of Jonathan's, along with assorted stagehands, musicians, and members of the crew, to Hurley's bar downstairs.

After several hours of laughing at nonstop Jonathan, they would simply have to go home, weak from mirth.

Carsey came to work one morning around 9 a.m. from New Jersey after one of these sessions and Jonathan was still there in Hurley's—in a manic phase—still "on" and still killing 'em.

Jonathan's improv versatility is legendary. Jack liked to surprise him on-air with an unexpected ordinary object, challenging, "See what you can do with this." A phone, a hat, a bucket, a billfold . . . whatever.

Robin Williams's fine piece in *The New York Times* on Jonathan told of the legendary Night of the Stick. Jack, perhaps thinking he might stump Jonny, handed him a two-foot plain stick of polished wood, and a classic was born. Instantly it became a fishing pole, Jonathan orally supplying authentic sounds of the reel and the splash.

Then, in rapid order, it morphed into about ten more things including a flute, a sword in the hands of an inept matador (who lets the bull get behind him), a violinist's bow drawn across his crooked left arm ("Think what I could do with the other part"), a golf club (as Jonathan magically transforms himself, with total vocal accuracy, into Bing Crosby), and a giant monster-movie beetle's antenna.

After some more transformations, suddenly it flies into his chest and, gripping the (now) spear that has fatally impaled him, he utters in a strangled voice, "The United Nations recognizes the delegate from Zambezi."

Seated now beside Jack and in mock annoyance at something Jack said, Jonathan turns the stick into a fairy's wand, wiggled at Jack with a mincing, "I make you vanish!"

Thank God for YouTube. It contains a trove of great Jonathan moments. The day Jonathan died, an inconsolable friend of mine canceled everything in order to spend the next day there, simply feasting on Jonathan.

Find "The Stick" and another Paar appearance when Jonathan, during an early stand-up, suddenly asks the viewers with solemn seriousness, "Did you ever undress in front of a dog?" If you fail to laugh at what follows, you may have expired.

He loved James Thurber and, like Groucho, idolized writers over performers. Both stated they'd have preferred to be revered more for their literary output than their performing. And both could write.

Virtually every obit used the word "genius." I suppose some

would be offended at using the same word that is applied to Mozart or Einstein for a mere entertainer. But to hell with those people. If Jonathan wasn't a genius, who was? Herbert Hoover?

I try to imagine someone who's reading this who never saw Jonathan and can't imagine, for example, what's funny about a white-haired old lady (Maude Frickert) in black bombazine and spectacles and old ladies' buttoned-up Enna Jettick shoes charging up out of Jack Paar's studio audience, pulling away from a man on the aisle who reached out toward her and reporting to Jack, "Did you see that? He tried to paw me!"

Jack: "I'm so sorry."
Jonathan: "Never mind, sonny, I'm a horny old chick!"

No familiar clichés for Jonathan. On one occasion, "Maudie" reported that a Mexican dinner had caused her the distress of "the green apple quickstep." And his invented names for his characters were perfect. For a rube, Elwood P. Suggins. A hick, Lester Cratchlow.

The sad part of Jonathan—I should say one of the sad parts—is that despite all that talent and all that greatness, his career was erratic, with short-lived *Jonathan Winters Show*s now and again, hundreds of hilarious guest appearances, and some mildly funny stuff in movies—a medium that couldn't accommodate his great improvisational talents. He was doubtless the greatest of improv comics, but not a great comic actor when bound to other people's scripted words. His film stuff is often uncomfortable and at odds with everybody else's style. His gifts lay elsewhere.

And nobody else had them.

APRIL 26, 2013

Missing: Jonathan Winters. Badly.

I remember once mentioning the name Jonathan Winters to Groucho Marx.

The reply: "There's a giant talent."

Among the pains suffered by Jonathan was an undeserved and unnecessary one. It was the up-and-down, here-and-there bumpy nature of his TV career. Not his great guest appearances, but actual *Jonathan Winters Shows*, which came and went, sometimes too quickly, over the years.

The terms "misunderstood talent" and "bum career management" circulated.

Herewith, a case in point.

One day I sneaked out of my *Tonight* office at NBC. "Jonny Winters is rehearsing in the next studio!" somebody whispered. I moved quickly.

It was the first of a series of specials in what was to be still another try at TV for him.

He had a hilarious routine he'd done, seated, on the Paar *Tonight Show* in which he created before your eyes an entire Western movie. A wagon train scene in which he was all the characters: wagon master, Grandma, dumb cluck, little boy, tongue-tied cowhand, outlaw, sissy sheriff, troubled cow, scared wild-stallion breaker . . . and more.

But this was prime-time television. Big budget. So what did the numbskulls do? They felt the need to "dress it up" for prime time.

They committed an artistic crime: a literal wagon train setting with a real covered wagon, a couple of uncomfortable live horses, bales of straw, milling extras, old ladies in sunbonnets and old gents sucking pipes, a small boy whittling, and . . . I can't go on.

In the midst of this, Jonathan enters, impeccable as usual in modern dark suit and tie, picking his way through the mob and the clutter to do his monologue. To refashion his imaginary but vivid world of characters while half drowned in distracting superfluities. A world created within his mind, more vivid than the literal one he was now in competition with. (His characters were always so perfectly drawn—with his ear not only for voices, dialects, and accents, but for regional, folksy terms and locutions.)

I wanted someone to charge down an aisle shouting "Fire the actors! Strike the set! Single spotlight on Jonathan! From the top!"

It was heartbreaking. Greatly talented performers don't know, often spectacularly, what's best for them, don't know what their talents really are and don't know what's just plain wrong for them. But somebody should.

People that remote from any perception of what Jonathan's talent was all about would probably suggest putting up a real glass wall for the mime Marcel Marceau to press his fingertips against. Or take down van Gogh's *Sunflowers* and put up some real ones.

I hope whatever alleged management and advisers on Jonathan's payroll allowed such a travesty to be inflicted on him have passed beyond the reach of my intemperate words. But I'd be tickled if they're seeing them. Are you there? Shame on you. Every man jack of you.

Needless to say, another Winters TV attempt was short-lived.

You could almost say the guilty deserved to be tied up and whipped, as Grandma was in the original Jonathan wagon train piece. "Lash 'er up there, Luke." With Jonathan's genius oral sound effects supplying the whish and snap of the bullwhip on the poor old lady. It was hilarious in the original verbal improv, neutered amid all the imposed, literal junk.

A book could be written about great talents who have been—to

the amazement and distress of almost everyone around them—
doggedly, self-destructively loyal to bad advisers and dull-witted
management types who truncate their careers.

Mental (bipolar) and alcohol problems also toughened life for
Jonathan.

It seems certain to me, in keeping with some bizarre Law of
Negative Compensation so often visited upon the greatly talented,
that the worlds of pleasure he gave to us far, far outweighed any he
was able to have himself. I hope I'm wrong. At least in degree.

I ran into him one day in a parking lot outside the Robin Williams *Mork & Mindy* studio. There was a slight awkwardness between
us because he was, oddly, never on my show, although he had said
he one day would be. I *feel* as though he was, and then I realize I'm
recalling the many Paar nights when I stood only a few feet from
him, off camera, drinking it in as Jonathan shone, bringing the studio audience to tears. And then reveling in it all again a few hours
later on the air.

An associate of his said he might have not wanted to go on with
me for fear of offending Johnny Carson. We were, after all, on opposite each other. That struck me as more funny than likely. Jonathan
and I were always cordial, and I'd forgive him anything. But the
regret is real. It just would have been so damn much fun to sit there
with him.

As we stood there in the parking lot, Jonathan began doing stuff
so funny that I felt guilty being the sole audience. I actually felt the
strong wish that unhappy folks and sick folks could be feeling the
tonic of this—at the risk of injuring themselves, laughing as hard as
I was.

He magically danced from character to character, then suddenly switched into still another one, and that very straight one
asked me, "Dick, did you ever think that Jack [Paar] was maybe
deep in the closet?"

As I see it, it was his "Jonathan Winters" character speaking.
The one I sensed he had devised to pass off in life as himself. Those

eyebrows up in the middle, the odd smile that sometimes showed only the bottom teeth and that sincere, friendly demeanor. I'm sure that Jonathan, like the half mad (or more) Peter Sellers, was always more comfortable when talking as somebody else.

I'm sure I've all but lost friends by maintaining that, despite their love for it, I always saw Stanley Kramer's *It's a Mad, Mad, Mad, Mad World* as more of an exercise in anticomedy than humor.

Of course, I loved Jonathan and the gas station in that film, but I've always deplored this lumbering heffalump of attempted humor that, "though it make the unskillful laugh, cannot but make the judicious grieve." (Bill Shakespeare, not Cavett.)

Chasing, crashing modern cars, no longer funny but ugly killing machines, unlike the funny, flimsy, almost butterfly-like, light-as-air "tin lizzies" of the silent days, showed a lack of sensibility that . . . Oh, forget it. Stanley Kramer was a nice man.

While making the thing, the lucky cast members were endlessly convulsed almost to illness by Jonathan between takes, in their trailers, and during meals. I know that any thirty minutes of those choice and lost improvised gems would outvalue a dozen *Mad, Mad, Mad, Mad Worlds*.

Someone else can now have the soapbox.

The Jack Paar appearances represent J. Winters's finest work, and however many survive should be preserved in a "Fort Knox of Comedy" vault. Surely I'm not the only one who remembers that Jonathan actually hosted *Tonight* for a full week back in the fifties, his cohost perched beside him: a live owl.

Where, NBC, is that lode of comedy bullion?

(My residential college at Yale had but one or two TVs in the basement. For the whole dorm. No student had a TV that I knew of. In order to see those great Paar appearances, my roommates and I would have to outnumber and edge out booze-soaked DKEs who preferred to watch wrestling or the Three Stooges.)

Typing this right now I keep being drawn, fondly, to the phone at my left elbow.

Earlier this year, Richard Lewis floored me, saying, "I talk to Jonathan on the phone every day." Assured it was true, I asked Richard for the number, got it, and a couple of months ago I called.

The familiar voice answered and my skin responded.

I heard, "Dick Cavett. My God!" and for the next hour was totally entertained as we reminisced about the old days and made each other laugh. He seemed much livelier than I'd expected, having heard how many illnesses he was coping with.

There were serious moments. He said he envied my having met Stan Laurel; that he worshipped Laurel and his work.

"Damn it!" he said with pained regret, "I'm the only one out here who never managed to meet him. And there he was, sitting right out there in Santa Monica all those years. The Oceana Apartments, wasn't it? I'll never get over that."

I was sorry that I told him that all that time, Stan Laurel was in the phone book. "Oh, Dick. You could have spared an old man that." (*Laughter.*)

Dept. of Self-Inflicted Pain: I resolved that in our next phone chat I'd tell him I would send him my two columns on meeting Laurel, deciding that two weeks would be a decent interval to call him again, but maybe shouldn't wait too long.

I did by three days.

The Richard Lewis–Jonathan Winters relationship is the stuff of a book or a big long article for a good magazine. Richard has granted me permission to include the following from an e-mail that followed my asking him about their unique friendship.

Here in that flowing, gift-for-language Lewis style is what he wrote.

> I talked to Jonathan almost daily on the phone when he was feeling well. In the past eight or nine years he must have left me hundreds and hundreds of insanely funny messages in my voicemail, each a different character and all gold. If I failed to mention the premise of his call I

was always touched when he asked me if I dug the bit. Imagine!? My childhood idol was asking me! We had a father-son comedy relationship. Both being recovering alcoholics we related on that level, Jonathan with a staggering fifty-three years sober before passing, and growing up we had a horrible time of it getting support from most of our family, diving into show business but mostly we free-associated in life and on stage and "got" the most obscure references from one another. He had special relationships with a handful of buddies that I know he treasured. We were his standing ovation every time we saw him or talked to him. (Every day.)

Do the book, Richard, with pages of those phone messages.

Why did this have to swim up out of memory? Part of my job with Jack was to spend one or two hours a week scanning viewer letters. A thankless chore. You are about to encounter the prizewinning dumbo one. It was from a woman in Cleveland who peppered the show with guest complaints. Ready?

> Dear Mr. Paar,
>
> Why do you keep having that Jonathan Winters on? He thinks he knows it all.
>
> Yours,
> Irene [Something]

Did I exaggerate? Might you not call this the cake taker of misapplication? The paragon of nitwittery? The Mount Everest of brain deficit? (The answer is yes.)

Sitting here, looking at that phone that the great man and I spoke on, random fragments of Jonathan keep surfacing in my head. One just did. It's only the first two lines that began a fall-down-funny sketch, showing how quickly and economically Jonathan could set and convey a scene and its theme:

Jonathan (*as motorcycle cop's siren*): *RRRRRRrrrrr* [and sound of braking]

Cop (*big, tough, surely homophobic*): Okay, buddy, where's the fire?

Jonathan (*sweetly*): In your eyes, officer. In your *eyes*!

There was Jonathan, and then there was everybody else.

MAY 10, 2013

Hel-LO! You're . . . Who Again?

It takes a certain amount of guts to go to your class reunions.

Particularly when your graduation ceremonies—from high school and from college—are about a half century back in time. There are too many reminders of "Time's wingèd chariot."

By the time I signed up for the first high school reunion I went to, I had become a "television personality." A fact that skewed the otherwise normalcy of the occasion.

I couldn't wait. What would my classmates' behavior be? Adoring? Awed? Fawning? Pointedly unimpressed?

Would I have the almost surreal experience of actually signing autographs for my *classmates*? (Yes.)

I blush now to recall how I fantasized what the impact would be of my grand entrance into a milling, partying crowd of those classmates. When it happened, the effect was enough to gratify even an excessive ego. I could immediately see, *"He's here!"* *"He came!"* and *"There's Dick!"* on numerous lips.

More confession, this one a bit cringe-making:

What I was feeling, irrationally and way too strongly, it took a moment to identify. It was: Why couldn't this famousness have been true back then, when I felt socially inept and awkward with girls? *Then* would Barbara Britten have gone out with me?

I was partly embarrassed by it all and partly struck with myself. I felt a bit like Bob Hope in a period comedy, stepping out of a carriage to an adoring crowd with "I wonder what the dull people are doing."

Not an entirely pretty sight, self-adoration-wise.

Working into the crowd at the Legion Hall—or was it a restaurant?—I tried to make eye contact whenever possible. When I was able to actually pluck a name from memory, the reaction was almost embarrassing.

I saw a guy named Berwyn Jones not far away and mouthed his first name through the din, an easy name to read at a distance. *"Yes!"* he mouthed back, pleased as punch. His delight was touching.

Of course there had to be at least one instance of the inevitable. A guy deep in his cups, with a redwood-sized chip on his shoulder, shoved at me a big glass of scotch: "I bought you this drink."

"A few sips of wine are my limit," I said politely.

"So I guess you're too damn good to have a drink with a nobody like me?"

Thank goodness, I suppressed anything like "You're not far from the truth" as his embarrassed wife led him away.

A surprising thing began to come clear. The girls I'd known long ago in school were now of two distinct sorts. Some of the prettiest had become with time, um, less so. But some who back then would have been, in the awful phrase, "desperation dates" had miraculously blossomed, with time. Into lovely and appealing women.

Time giveth and time taketh away.

A startling piece of news. One of the queens of my class—a beauty and a "big wheel" whom I had deemed a goddess too far above me by half to even speak to—had ended up a divorced mother of three, toiling as a waitress in a roadhouse café in Texas. My mind ran to Ecclesiastes' "Time and chance happeneth to them all."

Adonises from my class were fat and balding.

And I still felt inferior to them, as I had way back then. Until winning a state gymnastics championship assuaged any wimp factor floating about.

Quite a few Lincoln High reunions went by, at five-year intervals, before I ventured again.

This time, maybe a decade or so ago, there were only a couple of classmates in the registration room. One said, "You don't recognize us, but we know who you are."

Then I saw it.

A large bulletin board panel displayed rows of 8x10 photos of some of our classmates. The shock was immediate. They were those who had—as the world's favorite euphemism puts it—passed away. Even as a kid I wondered, is "passed away" better than being dead? Away to what? Or where? (I still wonder.) There was poor Tom H. and unlucky Ted P.—a car crash—and, oh, no! Not Sally L.!

Too many rows of them grinned out at us from their old, beaming graduation photos, faces full of life and eager promise.

Arriving at Lincoln's Cornhusker Hotel a little late for that night's big dinner, I was greeted by the cheery lady at the desk: "Mr. C., you'll find your classmates at the bottom of that escalator."

"Still standing, I hope," I said. I was Bob Hope again.

From just a little way down the escalator, looking at the people below entering the big dining room, I saw that the nice lady had clearly misdirected me.

There were several events in the Cornhusker that night, and this one was obviously one for old folks. An elderly wife helped a lame husband.

And yet there amid the elderly, was that not Karen Rauch, looking great as ever? What event was Karen attending with what looked like elderly relatives?

I didn't get it.

I ran the few steps back up against the tide of the torpid escalator and said to the woman at the desk, "I think you sent me wrong. That looks like a reunion of the Early Settlers Club."

"That's your class," she said. "I guess that's what happens."

Noticeable shock. Poetry came again. "Time, the subtle thief of youth" ran in my head.

These oldies were me, and I was them.

The strangest part of aging is that, as with suffering, people don't experience it equally.

A goodly number looked recognizably as they had in high school. Others, like those people's parents. The ages seemed to range a decade or more above and below what our common age really was.

It was as if the casting department had been told by a movie director, "I need a few hundred extras who graduated high school in the fifties. Throw in the usual number of good-lookers, some not so well preserved. And, of course, toss in a few shipwrecks."

Another bad moment. Some parents had been invited and I said to a man whose badge said, let's say, Jim Parks, "Young Jim and I were in French class together." His face changed.

You guessed it. This *was young Jim.* My brow hottens, just typing this. I've almost gotten over it.

There were side events, including a walking tour of our old high school. Seeing again the old corridors, lockers, and even drinking fountains exhumed long-lost memories. Like the time poor Leland (last name gone), during a fire drill, while the deafening siren drowned any talk or sound, decided to scream, *"Hi, Dickie!"*

I should have only seen, not heard, this. But in the instant between Leland's intake of breath and his deafening scream, the siren had stopped. His *"Hi, Dickie!"* had no competition. Leland seemed to shrink about five sizes. I was weak with laughter.

Every head turned as Leland was taken somewhere.

Suddenly, there was my picture. Part of an "L.H.S. Hall of Fame." My fellow "successes" were largely in business or state politics, I gathered—except for me and a pretty blonde. My friend Sandy Dennis—yes, that one. Also departed.

Now, sex.

I still can't reconcile my guiltless world in grades seven through nine, when sex was only rumored, at least for me. There's no avoiding "How times have changed."

In an earlier column I wrote about the variously worded newspaper headlines that year reporting, as one put it, "Fellatio on Junior High Bus—While Others Cheered." Would my Welsh Baptist minister grandfather—upon being informed what the key word meant—have expired on the spot?

Considering that naughty trick of Mama Nature's of endowing the male with his sexual peak at ages fourteen to eighteen, the question becomes why—with virginity now a rarity in high school—didn't way more than the few in my graduating class knock (or get knocked) up? Or did they? Keep your answer brief and to the point.

A group of us had opted for the tour of our old school's halls. The sharp young principal ultimately led us to a certain door in the "new section." It was inset and locked, so only a pair of people at a time could peer in the window.

Coming away, they looked puzzled.

My turn came. It was a room that looked like a large kiddies' toy store, all in bright colors with everything padded to prevent injury: tiny tricycles, fluffy, short ladders for climbing, and enough stuff to supply a sizable number of small people with playthings. People guessed at its purpose.

A woman asked if it was a nice charity project where poor kids could come and play.

I don't think anyone guessed the correct answer.

It was for the children of the students of Lincoln High School. There was a collective intake of breath.

Surely a boon for teenage day-care needers.

I haven't been to another L.H.S. reunion. I'm not sure why, but I have an odd theory.

Could it be an irrational fear of walking into that registration room on Day One and—in a moment out of *The Twilight Zone*—discovering my own picture on the "Those Who Have Left Us" wall?

(*Cue theremin music.*)

I thought I had finished with reunions. Years passed, and then . . .

"Are you going?"

"I'm not sure. Are you?"

My friend Chris Porterfield and I had tossed that ball back and forth for weeks.

Our Yale reunion.

Was it worth the increasing-year-by-year bad news of classmates and friends who were no longer with us? And of living ones to whom time and chance had happened . . . badly?

Of yakking, cocktail-quaffing classmates, even more boring than we remembered them?

Having endured the common but bitter shock of visual reminders of our advancing age at earlier reunions, both high school and previous college ones, we'd decided and hoped that enough fun could be conjured up to rate the time—and the expense—of going.

I arrived a day late. Checking in to the hotel, it was nice to see in the lobby a few unrecognized classmates with their name badges on. They looked remarkably fit. In a virtual sitcom moment in the elevator, I was on the verge of congratulating two of them. They were definitely fit. They were also, alas, from an appreciably younger class, also reuniting that week.

As with the high school reunion, the apparent age range of my contemporaries was dramatic. The changes in the Yale men were predictable: balding and acquired paunch. There was also a contrast between the gym-goers and those who don't. White hair was everywhere. (Mainly on heads, a comedian might say.) Is hair turning whiter sooner these days? Even at my earlier high school reunion, to look out from the stage over the crowd was to risk snow blindness.

Oddly, since we were Americans, I saw no shocking obesity. Most looked vigorous enough, with, here and there, a few walking wounded. Of course, who knew who had stayed at home?

Laughed myself silly at dinner with my old friend and classmate David Adnopoz. We had been a sort of team in plays, musicals, and scenes we did together for acting class, and we giggled foolishly, recalling the on- and offstage mishaps that had dotted our theatrical careers in those four wonderful years.

Deliciously, we recalled an event that, in an age of vastly less erotic opportunity than is readily available to today's young folks, had a whopping impact, never to be forgotten. The play was Schnitzler's *La Ronde*, which consists of a progressive series of seductions.

In one of them, a gorgeous, pulchritudinous actress, who went on to bigger things in theater and films, chose to play her scene moving about on her knees in a bed, nekkid from the waist up.

Deftly, E. (one of her initials) managed to cheat the unsuspecting folks out front of even a glimpse of her twinned treasury, but there was full view from the stage-right wings.

Somehow every male in the cast—and crew members who could leave their posts—managed to coincide nightly, crowding and pushing, in that dark stage-right wing for that scene.

I can recall nothing that has happened to me since more vividly.

Again, remember that this was the late fifties, when undergraduate male virginity not only existed but was, in appalling contrast to today, rampant. Without categorizing myself, I will say that this counted heavily in our appreciation.

I doubt that a comparable bunch of healthy young fellows of today would stand there, as we did, going quietly mad.

It must have been wicked fun for E. "Do you think E. knows that we can see her breasts every night?" one piping, beardless, callow youth asked.

"Guess," I said. Correctly.

Is it sort of sad in a way that such an adventure couldn't really happen today, now that every sexual aspect, perversion, position, and practice, normal and kinky, is—in living color and sharp focus— available to young folks of all ages from the time they're able to press computer keys?

I sometimes wonder how this may have affected the collective psyche. In those "old days" was there more or less sexual health? More or fewer batty Anthony Weiners and Bob Filners? I'd love to know.

Before the farewell breakfast on the sparkling, sunny last day there was a ceremony for the dead.

A chapel-like setting, a hundred or more attending. A brochure for the occasion contained the predictable shocks. Graduation photos with, ironically, lively and grinning faces of those who had died since the last reunion, five years earlier.

I opened the booklet of those who had joined the silent majority, hoping for a minimum of shock. And there was Jim.

He was one of my freshman year roommates. He'd written to me in Nebraska during the summer before Yale, announcing himself as a roommate-to-be and inviting me to his home in Bronxville, New York, for a day and night before motoring with his parents to New Haven.

(I just remembered that when Jim's telegram arrived in Lincoln, I saw that he had the same last name as a famous comedian. I hoped, in vain, that he was Jim's dad.)

On another sparkling, gorgeous day—all but unheard-of in New Haven, Connecticut—together, Jim and I stepped through Yale's Phelps Gate and into our new life.

His parents were always friendly and very nice to me, albeit a touch anti-Semitic. Jim, too. His wealthy Bronxville lawyer father noticeably so. This fact gave birth to a frequently remembered line in my earliest nightclub act, where I talked about all this. The line: "Bronxville has nothing to do with 'the Bronx.' (pause) Ever."

Jim was clever and we shared the odd gift of being able to ad-lib song lyrics with correct rhyming and scansion. More of a quirk than a gift.

Once, to the tune of "Davy Crockett" and a few beers, he improvised on the spot a song beginning, "Davy, Dave ben Gurion / King of the Hebrew Hordes." I recall fully only one couplet: "He's writing to business friends in the states / They're sending him rifles in gefilte fish crates."

A talent that might have been put to better use.

Jim came wobbling back to our room one morning freshman year, bleary from an all-nighter of booze and poker.

He had just had an epiphany, he said. "I realize, from last night, that I'm capable of something I shall never allow to happen. I shall never allow myself to get swallowed up in a swamp of irresponsible drinking, card playing, and debauchery. I shall not flunk out, sacrificing the ability to say, for the rest of my life, 'I went to Yale.'"

The "went" part became true some months later when Jim flunked out in his freshman year. Owing to the above-named vices.

I never saw Jim again, but I got one letter some years after graduation. He was living somewhere in Europe and announced his marriage. "I've changed a lot, as evidenced by the fact that I've married a Jewish girl. Mercy! What would Mom and Dad have said about their darling boy?"

At the memorial ceremony, as the names of the departed classmates were read, anyone who wanted to stood up and spoke about them. I told Jim's story. It got laughs and a nice approving murmur about his transformation.

A row of candles were lighted one at a time as each person was dealt with and spoken of. I can't have been the only person in that room wondering which of us might be candle-represented five years from now. Time to reread Philip Larkin's masterpiece on death, the poem "Aubade."

On the last night, in a big tent, we dined. And the Whiffenpoofs serenaded us. Against actuarial probability perhaps, all but a couple of the original fourteen members (from my class) of this great a cappella group were there.

They sang the famous song, the great pitch and harmony required for membership in that elite group—as part of which you got to tour world capitals—still intact.

Finally, we all stood, arms around waists, and all together, swaying from side to side, rendered the famous words and melody. Right from the opening line, "From the tables down at Mory's," there was lachrymosity among grown men.

I was sorry we didn't also sing the sentimental "Bright College Years," but I heard that it had been sung earlier at an event I'd missed. At the end of that old heart-tugger you take out your hankie and wave it in sync with the ultimate words, about how naught can avail "to break the freh-eh-end-ships formed . . . at . . . Yale." Much eye wiping was reported.

Yes, C. Porterfield and I decided, we were glad we went.

(We also agreed, emphatically, that we would like nothing more than to enter Phelps Gate again and do those golden four years over. Right through from the beginning.)

I guess the "cast" of any large school reunion will include certain stock characters: the Class Goof, still goofy; the Disappointedly Unremembered (a little acting required here); the Class Witless "Comic"; the Class Braying Jackass, whose intense, punishing, too-close-to-face conversation feels like a high-speed dental drill on an undeadened molar; the still-at-it, almost-ducked Class Religious Bore, still with his wretched tracts.

Oh, and the oily flatterer who causes you to be late for something while he describes and presses upon you the three-pound, four-hundred-plus-page manuscript of the allegorical play he has written, if that is the right word.

An item that, were there were still incinerators, would keep mine humming merrily.

Unpleasant moments are inevitable, but assuaged, in a wistful way, by things like the discovery of an opportunity missed; meeting someone delightful whom you didn't know and realize you very much wish you'd gotten to know, way back then.

Instead of some you did. Like the members, across the hall, of some fraternity, who somehow managed to stumble into our room just in time to vomit. (Is there one called DKE?)

Someone said at the close of the dinner, "We hope you'll all come back five years from now. Those who can"; looking as if he might have phrased that better.

It was early evening, getting dark, and while I stood on the Old Campus, looking up at the window of my freshman room, ruminating on ancient events there with my roommates Jim, Karl Muller, and Bob Leuze, a voice startled me from behind with "Hey, you Dick Cavett?" A tough, menacing townie, perhaps?

I couldn't make him out very clearly in the failing light, and for whatever reason I chose to deny it.

He went on, "Then how come you look so much like him? And sound like him?"

I said I didn't know. As he began to walk away, I thought why not give the poor guy a small thrill and said, "Okay, I am Dick Cavett."

"You wish," he replied, moving on.

June 14 & August 9, 2013

Good Night, Sweet Soprano

The sudden death at fifty-one of James Gandolfini is intolerable.

When he died, it never occurred to me *not* to go to his funeral. Until my wife pointed it out afterward, it also never occurred to me that I had "crashed" it. Standing in the sunshine in a long line in front of St. John the Divine I was spotted and we were ushered down front among family and colleagues.

My first mourner encounter was with the great Dominic Chianese (Uncle Junior). We embraced. The procedure, repeated over and over, while the church filled, was to come face-to-recognized-face with one *Sopranos* cast member after another, wet with tears, speaking not at all or with great difficulty.

And there they all were. I had, over the years, met most of them—Michael Imperioli, Steve Schirripa, Tony Sirico, Vince Curatola, Steve Buscemi, Vincent Pastore, et al.—and we exchanged hugs and kisses on the cheek.

(The unruly mind being what it is, the thought occurred to me that I hadn't been embraced and kissed by so many males since congratulating, backstage, the talented cast of a New Orleans drag show.)

So much crying. A grown man weeping is a tough thing to see.

There was a kind of through-the-looking-glass feeling standing there in a small group of Big Pussy, Paulie Walnuts, and Johnny Sack, plus, for seasoning, a noticeably reduced Governor Chris Christie. "Do you know all the Sopranos?" I asked him. "Most of them," he said. "And arrested some of them," the greatly gifted Curatola added, for a needed laugh. (It's no secret that the phrase "done a little time" applies to a cast member or two.)

The splendid Aida Turturro (Janice, Tony's sister) sensitively observed that what made it all so unbearable was that "Jimmy was just beginning to enjoy his life." He had turned down a movie this summer to finally spend some much-craved time in his vacation home on the water with his family.

As people still poured into the church, I went over to where Edie Falco and Turturro were sitting together, both dabbing tears. We spoke a little about how there's always something too anemic about the phrases people use in talking of mortality. Like the thread-bare euphemism "passed away." Preferable to dying, apparently, we sarcastically agreed.

Frighteningly, history will record that Edie Falco almost didn't get to *be* Carmela Soprano. She tells of how one more tiring audition seemed just too much that day, and besides, the show sounded, from the title, like some odd sort of musical production. But, lucky us, she did go, "and got the part of a lifetime."

What a wife she was to Tony and what richly complex characters they both were. And how miraculous that Nurse Jackie bears no more resemblance to Carmela Soprano than I do.

And I owe Edie an apology. Chatting, I misattributed to Hemingway a line from the great war correspondent Ernie Pyle's most famous and most widely reprinted column, on the death of Captain Waskow.

The dead officer was deeply loved by his men. All tears and grief, each one came up and stood by his corpse, laid out on the ground in the moonlight. One looked down and said, simply, "God damn it to hell, anyway." Pyle writes, "Then a soldier came and stood beside the officer, and bent over, and he too spoke to his dead captain, not in a whisper but awfully tenderly, and he said: 'I sure am sorry, sir.'"

It's strange, isn't it, how, in the presence of a dead person lying in the street, or one in a coffin at a funeral, you can feel for a moment not so much lucky as a little bit ashamed of being alive.

My last significant meeting with James—I'll get to the first in a moment—was in his dressing room on Broadway. My wife and I saw him in *God of Carnage*. Our front-row seats were so close to the stage you could lay your hand on it, and the light spill from the stage lighted me. Later in the dressing room, he said, "I kept seeing you. I almost said hello."

Then he described an attack of terrible anxiety that overtook him as beginning work on the play approached, with deep fears over—of all things—ability to learn and retain his lines. He said he'd actually entered a hospital for a few days of anxiety treatment. (Shades of Tony in Dr. Melfi's office.)

Meeting him, by the way, was initially a slight disappointment. Because he wasn't Tony. He didn't talk like Tony at all. He himself was no more Tony Soprano than Jackie Gleason was Ralph Kramden, or Jean Stapleton Edith Bunker.

He was an actor.

The subtlety, the darting bits of humor, the variety of facial and body movements and gestures, and especially the number of what you might call emotional and intellectual octaves available to this so richly gifted actor—too many wonders to gather and appreciate in a single viewing.

(David Chase, incidentally, probably owes the world the secret of how to produce episodes and, in fact, season after season of, to me, TV's best series. Whole seasons without a single—and I dare you to find one—dull moment. And cast to perfection. Not a clunker in that vast and varied troupe of splendid players. Chase might also reveal how you can mix humor and killing so expertly that the question has even been raised, was *The Sopranos* a comedy?)

Gandolfini's great feature was his eyes. For a man of unremarkable physique and features, the eyes were pure magic. They were soft, twinkly, cuddlesome, and loving. At other times, frozen, menacing, cruel, and murderous, shifting suddenly from one expression to another with startling impact. Those eyes were the outstanding, endlessly versatile feature of this gifted actor's arsenal of talent. He never made a false move.

Now: how I first met James. Years ago, in the midst of the series, a new friend, Michael Imperioli, Tony's problem nephew in the show, one day asked if I'd like to visit the set. It was among life's easiest decisions.

While standing on the sidewalk outside the studio in Queens, here Gandolfini suddenly came, strolling on break with Steven Van Zandt.

Not expecting to meet him so suddenly, I'd prepared no conversational gambit, coming up feebly with nothing more substantial than "Mr. Gandolfini, where I come from in Nebraska, your last name would be pronounced 'Gandol-*finny*.'"

He either politely showed, or skillfully feigned, interest in this pallid subject.

"The way my fellow Nebraskan, Johnny Carson, always said 'Hou-*dinny*' for 'Houdini,'" I added.

"Yeah, I've noticed that," he said, being a nice man.

Shooting resumed, he went away. And I felt the need to make a stronger impression on this hero of mine.

Inside, during a break, I'd been talking to a man in a martial arts T-shirt about the wonders of aikido and how I'd learned the "stunt" from a sensei in Tokyo of—by an almost mystical technique—making yourself unliftable. By anyone on earth. And how I had befuddled the giant footballer Mark Gastineau with it on TV.

I hadn't noticed Gandolfini passing by. "Did I hear you say you can't be lifted if you don't want to be?" he asked, politely, but brimming with skepticism. I admitted as much.

With about twenty cast and crew members watching, he, facing me, gripped me under the armpits, and lofted me up in the air as if I were a bed pillow.

I invited him to duplicate the feat. He resumed the grip, and with a mighty effort, grunting and groaning and with some perspiration, emitted a strained "Aarrgh!" and a guttural, "No way!" My feet never left the ground. There was good-natured jeering from the onlookers.

Afterward, some kind soul sent me a snapshot of the failed lifting moment. A puzzling picture of a large, tall man, oddly gripping a much smaller man's underarm areas for no apparent reason. (The large man is not as large as he later became.)

We did have one other, brief meeting, by pure chance. It was in the locker room at Wollman skating rink in Central Park. I'd gone there with a friend and he asked if I knew his friend Gandolfini. James, preparing to skate, greeted me warmly and said, "Thanks to you, all the guys on the set call me 'faggy' now because I couldn't lift Dick Cavett."

"Mr. Gandolfini, I almost *never* think of you as 'faggy,'" I offered.

"Thanks, Dick, I really needed that," he grinned. And, to the delight of the onlookers, rewarded me with a great big kiss.

John Donne reminds us that "any man's death diminishes me." James Gandolfini's sure did. He had so very much more to give us.

So long, James.

And God damn it to hell, anyway.

JULY 12, 2013

As Comics Say, "These Kids Today! I Tell Ya!"

The scene is a well-known Eastern college campus in the United States. A few weeks ago. Freshmen are arriving, many with parents but some alone, to begin one of life's greatly significant adventures. College.

And college life. With all that that entails.

Watching the arrivers and wondering if I could possibly have looked this young when transported from the plains of Nebraska to the world of ivy, I ask a student where a restroom is. I hate that word. As a precocious euphemism resister, I am supposed to have asked my grandmother at age six why you never saw anyone resting in there.

Anyway, there in the sleek, modern facility I checked out various notices taped to the walls. Useful information for the new student. Nothing very exciting. Then I saw it.

The Racy News.

I expected I'd discovered a student humor publication, tailored to the tastes of young folks and perhaps, judging by the title, of a slightly bawdy nature.

It would be hard to have been more wrong.

Dating myself by allowing some unruly element of prudishness to surface in me (old-fashionedness?), the mind rejected what it clearly was.

The subtitle: "Everything you ever wanted to know about effective consent." A clue hard to miss.

So what was the sheet about?

A vulgarian might blurt, when asked that question, "It's about screwing at school."

A more respectful description would be to call it a sensitive, respectful treatment of the fact that, unlike in my day, alas, with young people of college age today, sex is a feature of life. You'd have to be deeply mired in fogeyism to be shocked by the reality that sex-plus-campus is a fact.

And a fact vastly beyond what it was for those of us who were undergrads back in, and I hate to call it this, "olden times."

It goes on:

> [The college] sees unwanted sexual contact of any form as a violation of a student's personal integrity and his or her right to a safe environment, and is therefore a violation of our college's values and honor code. The college defines sexual misconduct as any sexual activity "without effective consent."

Let's assume, just for fun, that you are well past your college years. Did you have anything like that at your school?

The sheet is a product of a campus entity calling itself the Center for Sex and Gender Relations. The consent material is presented in such a way as not to sound like old folks talking to youngsters, so for example, "hooking up" is used instead of "intercourse." ("Hooking up" confusingly can also mean a range of activity from going together to the big bang itself.)

The sheet states, under "A Little Advice from Our Sexperts":

> It's your choice to engage in sexual activity! If you aren't ready, don't do it. It's okay to say no or wait.
>
> If you are ready, make sure what you are doing is safe and consensual.

It's okay to be nervous. It's natural. It's also pretty cute.

[I could do without the "cute" part.]

Don't rely on drunk hookups to get you by in college. Sure having a little fun once in a while isn't a problem . . . but we bet that you and your partner are better lovers sober!

They suggest telling your partner that you "haven't done that yet." That being a virgin is "not a mark of shame, and communication is the key."

Another section supplies dialogue suitable to the occasion. It states that it's "easy to get consent without ruining the moment." They recommend:

Can I kiss you here?
Do you like it when I touch you there?
How are you doing?
Should I keep going?
Does it feel better if I do it this way?
Are you into this?

Of course, a smart-ass could deface the poster with some suggested answers by witty young women to the above questions. Like:

Can I kiss you here? [No. Only in Cleveland.]
Shall I keep going? [Who knew you'd started?]

They also define "ineffective consent." Bad consent. It includes:

Silence.
No eye contact; pushing someone away.
Not asking simply because you've hooked up before.

Consent given for one sexual act does not mean that
your partner is consenting to everything.

Given when under influence of alcohol or drugs . . .

God, how I wish my college years had had something like that.
My guess is that the amount of sexual activity on campus back then
would be at about a ratio of thirty to one. (The "one" being my
"then.")

I don't want to embarrass my former roommates, so I'll use no
names, but I'm fairly sure I was the first and perhaps for a while
only one of us to bid virginity good-bye as an undergrad. And it
wasn't until my sophomore year. (It was awkward and without distinction.)

A long wait. And, to quote Miss Bette Davis on a show of mine,
when I impulsively inquired about her own virginity, "The wait
damn near killed me!"

All of this makes me feel quaint. It's hard to read and think
about it without remembering the pains of that less liberated time. I
can't help wondering how different a person I might be if I'd had the
benefits of the present age, where sex is not a big deal. Just one of
many things you do. Where sex imaginable and unimaginable is
available on your computer screen. Including *"Live* from Sweden."

Would I have had a different character or outlook on life if my
school years had been adorned—as school years are today—with
regular pleasurable hot-bedding in college, high school, and, as we
are repeatedly told, junior high?

Mother Nature's nasty little trick of giving the male of the species
his sexual peak roughly between ages fourteen and eighteen was
particularly hard on my contemporaries when getting into someone's underthings—and I don't mean wearing them—was something
you didn't do on pain of death.

How wonderful if there had been available relief of a two-person
(at least) sort. If only so you could concentrate on your studies and
dream about something else for a change. And those godawful

necking sessions, pleasant for a while, but resulting, for the male, in a crippling case of azure gonads. (I believe there was another term.)

Mightn't today's way have made me a much happier and maybe even better individual?

You tell me.

SEPTEMBER 13, 2013

More Sex, Anyone?

You made me laugh. You, the reader who wrote that, on the subject of sex before marriage, your mother asked your father the farthest he had gone with his before-marriage girlfriend. "Poughkeepsie," he replied.

My last column inspired a remarkable number of thoughtful replies. I wish I had space and time to deal with all of them.

The college I wrote about that posted information and advice on sex at school is, I learn, hardly unique. And many readers wonder what took so long. If only we had had that as a theme.

Only a handful could be considered shocked or disapproving of the practice. Many worried about the possibly lost distinction between sex and true affection.

I am always shocked that there are still a handful of defenders of the dubious practice of abstinence, surely the worst idea since chocolate-covered grasshoppers. Or Dick Cheney.

Undoubtedly this sometimes reliable practice urged on the young, combined with forbidding them contraception, has accounted for a hefty portion of the income of the baby-shower industry.

Abstinence. What sex-drive-free human specimens dreamed this one up? Were, or are, they utter strangers to the turmoil of the storming erotic drives of the young? And, as several fortunate readers attest, some lucky members of the old?

If there is an Abstinence League, my image of its leader comes from William Blake's "Proverbs of Hell": "Prudence is a rich ugly old maid courted by Incapacity."

Remember when the "one true church" was heavily promoting the "rhythm method" of pseudo-contraception? Of course the jokes came thick and fast about inability to keep a beat, etc. I still wonder what wit first labeled the fiasco "Vatican roulette." A daredevil version, it proved to be, of roulette with about four chambers loaded.

I liked the reader who admitted quite frankly that, yes, she did think additional sex experience would have been a good thing in her case, probably producing a more successful marriage.

Several people referred, or at least alluded, to the danger of a wrecked school life and education from an unwanted pregnancy.

No small concern. More so in my day, when detailed knowledge of the traps and pitfalls of the loins was often sparse.

I received zero sex knowledge at home. Had my mother lived, I might well have, but my dad merely worried that I was going to impregnate someone in high school. But no advice. No instruction.

Considering the thinness of my sexual activity at the time, the odds against the calamity that haunted A. B. Cavett were somewhere below zero. I wouldn't be surprised, such was the extent of my dad's concern, to learn that he might have had some such related experience himself.

In college, where the odds favoring inadvertent calamity at least climbed to just *above* the freezing point, I can still recall a stabbing and chilling moment of angst, fear, and trembling.

The previous night had included a rare episode of pneumatic bliss, properly conducted, safety-factor-wise.

The next day, as chance would have it, Fate, or one of my roommates, placed in my hands one of those pamphlets for boys. It at least *felt* as if my hair stood up at reading the icy words: "Be careful not to touch the end of your penis to the wrong side of the condom, then turn it over and . . ."

It went on to make it clear that the not inconsiderable frequency of this inadvertent "transfer" mishap could account, accidentally, for an addition to the population.

At that, the black-and-white tile floor of the dorm bathroom where I was standing seemed to zoom up at me as in an early film noir special effect.

Had I done that? Had I wrecked my life? Cold sweat.

Was there a preacher in my immediate future? Would I be on a train back to Nebraska? Would I be home, saying "Hi, folks. Meet Janie"?

For a good time thereafter, sleep was fitful and sometimes impossible without a mild sleeping potion and a page-or-two dose of Spenser's *The Faerie Queene*—a sure-fire soporific.

Why tell this? As an argument for sex education? Surely no one with a measurable IQ is still against that, although in fact you can still hear folks with but ten watts upstairs say, "Why put ideas in kids' heads?"

My wondering about whether more sex in school, in my part of the Olden Days, would have made me a better person seemed to divide the audience.

I was assured it would have and that it emphatically would not. I suppose all we can say here is, how will we ever know?

Some readers made the distinction of how different things always are for boys and girls. A female reader, disputing assumptions about the time, wrote of the incredible pressure "in the 60s even" for girls to "keep your knickers on" or be looked down on by female classmates. But that now, she says, the pressure is to "lighten up, get with it." To shuck 'em.

She feels the school's enlightened document I quoted is spot on.

Some urged that doleful term "waiting," maintaining that "character" is built by biting the bullet and *waiting*.

Poppycock.

The great Marlene Dietrich told me that in her German upbringing, she was commanded to go without a drink of water when thirsty "to build character." Did it? I asked. "Not one brick's worth of character was built. It probably injured my kidneys."

One reader, Joe of Brooklyn, touchingly wonders if, as a schoolkid, that certain gorgeous dream of a teacher ever fancied him, envying those fifteen-year-old students these days taken "twixt the sheets by a comely and passionate high school teacher." (Who subsequently does time.)

Poor Joe has never gotten over it. He thinks in today's atmosphere, the "it" he longed for just might have happened. She was thirty-three then—she would be ninety-two now—and "she is still more enticing than any other woman I have ever encountered."

Joe says every man he tells this to has a similar schooldays story and longing. I know I do. Would we have been better off? Anyway, Joe, you have at least a sitcom episode here, if not the core of a feature.

Glad that so many writers liked the column and applauded the school's efforts, warnings, and advice about that old devil, sex. Many wish they'd had it. Such a document, I mean, of course.

(A few practical souls pointed out that it is also greatly in the school's legal interests to be able to say to thundering parents, "We told them.")

Predictably, I guess, I was taken to task (what in hell does that really mean?) by some readers for committing humor within such a topic. This always puzzles. The old "There is no place for humor here."

You have it almost right. There is no place for *no* humor. At what boundary must humor halt? I commend you to my friend Mark Twain on the power of humor: "Against the assault of laughter, nothing can stand."

As further assertion of the place of humor being everywhere, let us close with the wise, wise advice about life given by the great George S. Kaufman to his young daughter Ann.

"Sample everything in life. Except incest and folk-dancing."

OCTOBER 11, 2013

Tough Way to Lose a Friend

Every writer knows that unless you were born gifted with either supreme confidence or outsized ego, handing in your work holds, in some cases, admitted terror. If that's too strong, at least fairly high anxiety. Even if what you wrote seems unusually good to you, part of you is vulnerable to the suggestion that you may have laid an egg. A bad one. As W. C. Fields might have put it as your editor, "Sadly, my little lad, you have contrived in this instance to produce a specimen of odoriferous hen fruit."

Sometimes you don't realize the degree of your insecurity until you get back those warming words from an editor-type person. The simple "Nice one" warms the doubting heart. Even just "Nice" is eagerly embraced. "Good one" does wonders.

But there's one comment I never expected to get, but did last week.

"We really can't publish this."

Reading on, through rapid heartbeat came the kindly meant "Don't worry. It happens when you've written so many . . ."

I had written that column before.

It was about a time in Hollywood, years ago, when—with perhaps too much interest in the legendary imbibers the Scott Fitzgeralds—I decided to try getting monumentally drunk.

Being in show business, I've encountered drunks of every stripe. Often funny, usually sad, some tragic.

I don't *get* being a drunk.

One of my best friends, colleagues, and just an all-around

delightful person to be with was a drunk. He—Tom—and my late friend Pat McCormick, sometimes together with Jonathan Winters, would improvise hilariously, backstage at the Jack Paar *Tonight Show*, or in Hurley's legendary bar, or on the sidewalk, convulsing a swelling crowd.

I loved them collectively and individually. They were all drunks. All were, in that selected euphemism for being one, "recovering alcoholics."

Tom was somehow the saddest. Jonny and Pat got it under control. Tom, intermittently.

Having worked all over television, most notably for Paar and for Allen Funt on *Candid Camera*, Tom was a sweetheart: amiable, genuinely funny, a good, good friend, and a fanatical Chicago-accented Cubs fan, sticking with them through thin and thin.

When Tom delighted me by joining my PBS show staff, it was cause for (alcohol-free) celebration. He was the leading master, from years with Jack, of the art of preparing a guest, big or small, for appearing on a talk show. He should have published his techniques. I once heard him say to a guest he was prepping, "Now say the last line of that story in the same words and the same way you just told it to me. Leave out the word 'very' before 'embarrassing.' It'll get a bigger laugh." He was always right. Everyone liked him. And I liked his frankness in letting my producer know that he knew his drinking reputation preceded him. My producer was frank in return. Reassurance from Tom came in the form of a single bit of information. Tom's doctor had told him if he drank again he'd die, so great was the physical punishment already self-inflicted. Things went nicely for a good long while.

Then, the first troubling signs. Nothing blatant, just an odd habit of vanishing from the office at odd times.

And then other signs.

We all suspected Tom had slipped off the wagon. Distressed, I suddenly surprised him in an otherwise enjoyable phone call full of humor: Tom, if you're drinking now and I asked you for the truth, you'd deny it, wouldn't you? A long pause. "Yes."

Ron Fried, the author and television producer, including for me, was back then a lowly PA (production assistant) on my staff. The trouble grew, and Ron got it firsthand.

Tom got spooked somehow about some show problem. At an early morning editing session, he asked Ron to smell his breath. Ron noticed its two main ingredients: "Chewing gum . . . of course! . . . and booze. I didn't tell him." I doubt that I would have either, though I'm not sure why.

During one of Tom's absences, Ron was sent to his home to pick up notes. Tom, he said, looked as if he had been in a fight and did not want that fact reported. One day at work he, with a lame excuse, sported a comic-strip black eye. That standard stock character, the boozing, brawling Irish drunk with a deteriorating liver, was an image Tom loathed while, on occasion, exemplifying it.

It fell to my producer at the time, Chris Porterfield, to deal with the problem. It was no fun for any of us. He and I think I may have been the one to suggest calling the wonderful Malachy McCourt, actor, popular barkeep, restaurateur, and good friend of Tom's. Malachy—and I hope he won't mind being called an expert on the subject—was terse.

After we ran through a number of "signs"—chewing a lot of gum, keeping his office door closed, sudden disappearances, uncharacteristic errors, sloppiness in his work—Malachy knew.

I remember his chilling assurance that, all those signs being present, "You might have to remove the grill on the ventilator in his office to find the bottle that is surely there."

I'm pretty sure Malachy said that the word for how to treat the situation was "brutally." His advice was to corner him. Not by literally blocking the door but by *knowing* he was drinking, allowing no argument on that point, and saying what had to be done.

To spare embarrassment, the staff and others could be told Tom was taking a two weeks' or so vacation. He would, without argument or denial, enter treatment. I think it was St. Vincent's detox program.

In what would be considered a good actor's or director's touch in a performance, Tom suddenly covered his face in both hands. Was he going to cry? Throw a punch? Either was possible. Instead, he simply spoke.

"God. This is so . . . *humiliating.*"

Perhaps the doctor was wrong. Tom didn't die. Or not just then. Staff memories have dimmed on what followed Tom's treatment at St. Vincent's. He did come back in good shape. He may have fallen again.

When that show ended I lost touch with Tom for a long stretch of time. Then I heard he was dead.

I wish I understood the workings of the alcoholic mind. While taping in San Francisco, Robin Breed (one of my producers), Chris, Tom, and I went for a daytime stroll in the sunlight. Tom was sober then. On a corner was an inviting-looking cocktail lounge bar. Tom said, "Wouldn't it be wonderful to just spend the whole afternoon in there, drinking whisky sours?"

No one responded. Had it been a cartoon, three "balloons" would have appeared over our heads, each bearing the word "No." And not meaning no you can't, but no it wouldn't.

If you're an alcoholic in show business, you're at least in good company—the Burtons, Sinatra, doubtless Judy, and enough more that the list would extend this piece another page. And, surprisingly, *not* Dean Martin, I'm told.

I guess I'm undeservedly lucky, whether it's my genes or that my swimming-pool booze binge in the twice-written article and, mainly, the hangover that would have killed an ordinary man inoculated me against a life of tippling.

The German for an awful hangover is *Ein furchtbarer Katzenjammer.* And that's just how it feels.

When I think of the aftermath pain that next morning, it

reminds me of a line in Johnny Carson's socko nightclub act. A line written for him, I'm sure, by my late friend David Lloyd. Johnny said this line got the biggest obvious identification laugh from the sadly experienced in the audience. About the next morning agony, he said, "Your hair hurts and you can't make a fist."

I wonder what strange brain quirk just popped a line from somewhere in Shakespeare into my head:

"Poor Tom's a-cold."

NOVEMBER 15, 2013

Cavett on Booze, Again

Judging from your e-mails and from other in-person comments, it seems to be a rare thing not to have been touched by problem drinking somewhere among family or friends or business associates.

Web sites on alcohol and drinking statistics abound. Numbers vary, but clearly millions are suffering the tortures of the damned. No less an authority than Don Imus, sober for long years with the day-at-a-time method, having read the last column, imparts the sad news that "rehab works for one out of four." Every bit as disturbing is the statement of a highway patrolman I know that one out of five drivers heading toward you—or your kids—in the oncoming lane on Friday and Saturday night is over the intoxication limit. Or, less politely, drunk. One Saturday night, traveling east on Long Island, my car became the fifth in a line of cars to peel off into the right-hand ditch rhythmically, one after the other like Rockettes, as a speeding oncomer decided he preferred our lane.

One Web site puts the number of people deeply suffering at 15 *million*. Keep that in mind when those weekend cars come at you.

I all but forgot that years ago, in my early days on ABC, I did a two-part show on alcoholism. Standing out most clearly in memory is an attractive, intelligent, well-spoken mother of three who survived shooting herself in the forehead while drunk.

Readers made the point that "too smart to be a drunk" cuts no—pardon the expression—ice.

It's a shame that such a heavy price is paid by both the drinker and his victim for a substance that is so wonderful in its good ways: a lubricator of conversation, a steadier of nerves, a remover of that little edge of anxiety, an uninhibitor of the lover. And the lovee. In movies, anyway, a steadier of the trembling hand of the drunken doctor, usually played by Thomas Mitchell.

(Though of course loss of inhibition, pushed too far, can release the inner rapist as well.)

I wish I'd discovered earlier that with my weak head, a mere tablespoon's worth of wine before going on took away that annoying little edge of performance nerves.

For a while I felt guilty about this, or about recommending it. Would that make me an enabler? The greats don't need a drink, I thought. (I was very young.)

Then one night, backstage at *The Tonight Show*, I saw Jack Benny— yes, *Jack Benny*—seemingly the calmest, most assured, and relaxed man in all of show business, quite casually call for and down a couple of inches of scotch, with one ice cube, before sauntering with that wonderful walk calmly onto the set with Johnny. I stared in disbelief.

I appeared on the old *Kraft Music Hall* with George Burns. Just before airtime I was nervous as hell. George came to my dressing room and offered me a snort from his hip flask as if that were traditional. Brace yourself: I held it in my mouth, nodding thanks, and as he left I spat it into the dressing room sink, terrified that I would come reeling onto the stage. Dressing room sinks, time out of mind, have served multiple purposes.

(Remember George Gobel's rationale for taking a stiff drink before going on? "You don't expect me to go out there *alone*, do you?")

The world of showbiz has always had a heavy population of drunks. Fine actors like Jason Robards, Bogie, Maureen Stapleton, Trevor Howard, most Barrymores, Veronica Lake (drunk on my show), Robert Newton, Dana Andrews (reportedly needing to have his head held in a brace for close-ups), Dick and Liz, Peter O'Toole, and Robert Mitchum represent a tiny percentage of the showfolk apparently plagued with "the cup that cheers." And how did I leave out the great Spencer Tracy, who suffered alcohol *seizures*, bellowing and hurling furniture and glassware and having to be needled by a doctor into unconsciousness?

Burton's vivid eloquence on my PBS show on what it is to be the slave of alcohol was recalled by readers, some of whom found it on YouTube, I think. Obviously people vary in their capacities. Mitchum explained, in one of two wonderful shows I did with him, that he could drink large quantities of alcohol with no apparent effect of any kind. Hardly a blessing, liver-wise, I should think.

I told an AA friend of mine that by just licking the surface of a martini—not even taking a sip—I can feel it down to my toes. He paled, saying, "My God, I had to drink three to feel *anything!*"

He's the same one who told me a profound thing that sticks with me, certainly in relation to Tom of my "Tough Way to Lose a Friend" column. He said, "An alcoholic is so devious, he will even quit drinking to prove he's not an alcoholic."

We needn't recite the list of famous alcoholic writers that usually starts with Hemingway and Fitzgerald and Faulkner.

John Cheever said he could drink anywhere, anytime, except when working. I'd asked, "Does drink help writing?" His negative reply was wonderful: "I can detect a sip of sherry in a paragraph."

Tom (of the previous column) had worked on many television shows and I'm not sure if my producer was the first or even the last to have to can him—as Tom himself had requested when coming aboard, if he tumbled from the wagon. My producer needed a bit of a nip himself after performing the hateful deed.

Tom was affable, wittily funny, and a hilarious storyteller. One day he came to work lamenting, once again, the gentrification of his beloved Columbus Avenue. He complained that he had just seen a new funeral parlor named "Death 'n' Things."

Strangely, I saw myself as an exception to the apparent rule that everyone has a drunk somewhere in their family. At first I could think of none. Then, in an eerie procession, they began to file into consciousness, coming into focus like ghosts in a story.

Here came Aunt Betty, a gorgeous blonde on my stepmother's side who made a total mess of her life and family. My somewhat saintly stepmother somehow collared all of Betty's bewildered grade-school-age kids, brought them to Lincoln from St. Louis while their mom was particularly bad, and gave them a birthday party. They'd never had one.

When she inevitably lost the kids, and kicked the booze well after her divorce, she got by on two other addictions. Chain-smoking and crappy television jewelry, which she ordered incessantly, saying, "I need this. It keeps coming in, making every day a birthday." Not all of her wits survived the booze. When she died, from smoking, all the drawers of her desk were found stuffed with the shiny junk frippery. Most of it unopened.

Smoking, sadly, seems to be the favored other addiction of the alcoholic. Before being recognizable, I was sneaked into an AA meeting with a friend. You could barely see the walls for the cigarette smoke, with coffee consumed by the gallon.

Speaking of writers, I once drove the Pulitzer Prize winner Jean Stafford (the former Mrs. Robert Lowell and also the former Mrs. A. J. Liebling, as well as my late wife's and my great friend) to her home in East Hampton. She was asleep, drunk, in the passenger seat. Suddenly she stirred and in her beautiful, almost baritone voice said, "I hate it. I hate alcohol. It is my seducer. And my enemy." And went back to sleep.

I'm at a loss for how to close on this unclosable subject. I think I'll let one of the readers have the honor. From "geomurshiva of cooperstown, ny":

> Being a critical care nurse for a long time, I have seen
> what alcohol can do to any one of us. We think most
> often of the long term drinker and the liver failure and

the disorientation and the sad last days of coma and the family at the bedside crying so sadly for the loss of another life to booze. Thanks, Mr. Cavett, for the good read. . . . But, for most of us serving the sick we cry more for the younger ones who got drunk at a college party and then went driving only to die in a car crash or sustain brain injury and paralysis. . . . These victims of alcohol are forgotten all too soon. They become statistics only. Alas.

JANUARY 10, 2014

Only in My Dreams?

T hose damned anxiety dreams again.

While you're writhing and twisting in the bedclothes, dreaming that you're late, never going to get there, everything gets in your way, your stuff's all over the room, you'll never get packed in time for the plane, your legs and arms aren't even working right, and, and . . .

With a shudder, you're awake. Relief. You may even say aloud, "Thank God that was only a dream."

But it felt worse than if it had been real, and you remember, again, Freud's observation that the psychic pain in dreams exceeds what the same situation would feel like in waking life.

There are disturbing dreams, painfully troubling dreams, and there are nightmares. I don't, but some have dreams of hideous, pursuing monsters, thirsty vampires, slimy and enveloping webs of giant spiders. My anguishing dreams are invariably that I'm ill-prepared, not ready, and will make a fool of myself: in the play, in the speech, in the exam. And the pain of these seemingly mundane situations is a torture the CIA might envy.

A few of mine are more elaborate, with more exotic settings. How would you categorize the following?

The setting: Clothing and other clues tell us it's somewhere in the mid-eighties. You are on a large, seaworthy river cruise ship, deep in China. You and your mate have opted to skip the next stop's two-hour side trip to contemplate yet another essential temple.

Yes, my temple quota had been reached. And exceeded.

I opt to strike off on my own. I can step into nearby China and enjoy being unrecognized. I get the name of a picturesque small town not too far away and am taxied there, past miles of fairly dreary landscape and endless telephone poles.

I'm enjoying that strong, fun sensation you can exult in when in a foreign country: nobody, at this moment, has any idea where I am. Including me.

(*The scene shifts now. Chinese restaurant. Interior.*)

Now I'm at a restaurant table trying to find a bite or two of edible substance in a bowl of some kind of alleged salad featuring sharp, broken hunks of chicken bone so undercooked that they exude pure raw blood.

The waitress sees my displeasure. She has no English and I waste upon her, "This isn't food, it's attempted homicide."

Departing through the beaded curtain, I flash back to Saturday afternoon serial days, wondering if, behind me, a dark, pigtailed figure will fling a dirk drawn from the back of his collar across the room, expertly implanting it between my shoulder blades.

As I step outside and look around the alien landscape, the thought that was no doubt unconsciously accumulating bursts into consciousness and hits me between the eyes.

I have let my cabdriver go! I don't know how we got here. There are dozens of roads. I don't know where the ship is docked! I don't know the ship's name. There may be dozens of piers. And dozens of ships, one with my wife on it. And all of them without me. Oh, God!

(Typing and reliving that moment just caused a noticeable increase in pulse rate.)

Have I been fooling you a little up to this point by seeming, perhaps, to be describing a dream? Alas, dear reader, this was stark reality. This bloody well happened. And, worse, not to someone else.

To have no language available to you is an awful thing.

Japanese is sort of a hobby of mine and I can get around Japan with ease. But there is no Japanese in Chinese. And little English in the part of China I had chosen to strand myself in with a ship leaving.

(Oh, and the cell phone, young people, wasn't yet ubiquitous at the time of this particular adventure. There were a few so-called mobiles around, but they were more the size of a phone booth than a phone.)

And what kind of brains? Really!

Is this the same person who, as someone surprisingly wrote in an article about me, had "the highest IQ of anyone ever to go through Prescott School in Lincoln, Nebraska"? If true, would that person be dumb enough to get himself hopelessly lost in China? And what else might he be dumb enough to do?

We'll soon find out.

Desperate for communication, and sweating, I clumsily tried to convey my plight to a couple of (other) cabdrivers—when, suddenly, a glimpse of salvation.

There was Larry King.

Three feet away, on a store window TV screen, was Larry, from the good old U.S.A. I was saved. Larry's live. I'll call him somehow and he can tell the Chinese where I am and . . . The irrational brain paused there, and subsided. Temporarily.

Back to the two drivers. Through a combination of clumsy charades and a crude drawing of a ship, hope glimmered. One man said the Chinese equivalent of "Aha!" (That may be exactly what he said. Is it universal?)

Although hope had glimmered earlier as well, when I pulled from my pocket something that might have the ship's name on it. Yes, it was ship stationery. But the top, with the printing, was torn off.

The gods were toying with me ruthlessly.

But the one driver seemed confident. Some words had been recognized, it seemed. Maybe "cruise ship." As I hurtled along in his cab, the telephone poles looked familiar. But then, don't most telephone poles? I saw no land that supported a body of water.

And I had no idea how much time we had. I'll forgive you for failing to believe that, on top of everything, my watch had stopped. Not that it mattered. It seemed nothing did. Life was pretty much over.

Honestly. The absurdity of it.

I have—or should it be *had?*—a lovely cabin on a lovely ship on a lovely vacation and I've gotten myself lost in an antique land, without a clue about how to get rescued.

What if the ship's gone? Where do I go? People recognize me almost anywhere, but not here. I think of the line "My face is my passport." Now, only my passport is my passport. My face has expired.

Whatever "hoping against hope" can possibly mean, that's what I was doing. But on what evidence? Maybe the driver had totally misunderstood. More telephone poles. He might be speeding me farther inland. To a Chinese rodeo.

And then, wonder of wonders. Coming down a hill, I can see first the tops of some masts ahead. And then—the ship. About half a mile away. And not moving.

An odd quirk occurs in my half-ruined brain. I now see my thoughts in block letters. In that short, blunt, constipated style that the Hemingway typewriter produced so readily:

"It is a ship. It is a good ship. It is a good ship for it is my ship." (Sorry, Ernie.)

We pulled into a parking lot as close as possible. About twenty yards from dockside. The ship sounded its whistle.

It began to move.

I hurled all the paper money I had at the driver—possibly a year's salary for him—and ran for it.

The rational brain said not to do anything foolish. Then the irrational one took the controls:

You were a champion gymnast once. You can leap for that railed deck at the back end (stern?).

Thoughts, thick and fast and jumbled. "If I miss and land in the drink surely somebody will—" What? Take off his (or her) shoes and what? And there isn't anybody.

I don't want to overdramatize this heroic feat. The ship was not speeding along. It was lumbering. But there's no getting around the fact that the correct phrase for what I was dealing with would be, let's face it, a moving ship. I would have preferred stillness.

Channeling Errol Flynn, I took to the air and landed easily enough, hanging there on the outside of the ship's rail like a kid hooked by his armpits over a baseball field fence.

I scrambled fully aboard. And here's the sad part. There was not a single witness. No cheering spectators, no videocam, no applauding and adoring females. Nothing.

Now I was to learn what had happened. My wife, napping, had been awakened by an announcement. "We are leaving in ten minutes. Will passenger Cavett please identify himself." She assumed I had.

Did they also assume so?

I didn't blame them for not holding everybody up for one fool.

Yet a friend of mine, not unfamiliar with the law, said, "You should have sued them. Knowingly leaving a prominent passenger, or any passenger, stranded and abandoned? No way."

Hmm. Is it too late?

Advise.

Finally, what can we learn from this, boys and girls?

Two things: (a) don't ever, ever get lost in foreign lands, and (b) leap for boats only when it's wise and sensible.

DECEMBER 14, 2012

Acknowledgments

George Kalogerakis, my editor at *The New York Times*, for invaluable help rendering my offerings into presentable reading form and, when necessary, for keeping me from going over the top. (And on occasion, too far under it.)

Paul Golob, formidable presence at Henry Holt, for his sharp, sharp eye and his skill in shepherding these columns from the digital world onto the printed page.

Lisa Troland, whom I'm urging to get rich writing "How to Be the World's Greatest Assistant."

And, lest I forget, my wife, Martha, whose talents and virtues, listed, would fill the rest of this page. (Even in small print.)

Index